THE **PRODIGY**

Adventures with
the Voodoo Crew

To Tansey and Ruby Blue

THE PRODIGY

Adventures with
the Voodoo Crew

Martin James

EBURY
PRESS

First published in Great Britain in 1997

1 3 5 7 9 10 8 6 4 2

© Martin James 1997

Ebury Press
Random House, 20 Vauxhall Bridge Road, London SW1V 2SA

Random House Australia Pty Limited
20 Alfred Street, Milsons Point, Sydney, New South Wales 2061, Australia

Random House New Zealand Limited
18 Poland Road, Glenfield, Auckland 10, New Zealand

Random House South Africa (Pty) Limited
Endulini, 5A Jubilee Road, Parktown 2193, South Africa

Random House UK Limited Reg. No. 954009

A CIP catalogue record for this book is available from the British Library

ISBN 0 09 186088 1

Cover photo Laura Wickenden

Back cover photograph Retna
Back cover photograph of Martin James: Mark Stringer

Printed and bound in Great Britain by Mackay's of Chatham plc

Papers used by Ebury Press are natural, recyclable products made from wood grown in sustainable forests.

Acknowledgements

First and foremost I would like to thank The Prodigy: Liam Howlett, Leeroy Thornhill, Keith Flint and Keeti Palmer, aka Maxim Reality. Without their co-operation, this project would have been a very different adventure indeed. Liam, I would like to thank for your endless interest and enthusiasm in the book. For inviting me round, making me feel welcome at the gigs and generally putting up with me calling every other day for another little chat. Oh, and for always saying, 'shit, you'd better not write about that!' Leeroy, my gratitude goes out to you for being there with the stories, the jokes and just a touch of madness. You may be an Arsenal fan but you're still a top geezer in my book – one of these days I'll sort you out on a one-on-one at Rage Racer! Flinty, for those five-minute phonecalls which always took over an hour, and the frank and honest things you had to say. Keeti – for making me laugh, for making me feel uncomfortable (that stare, man!) and for coming up with the goods when I was up against it.

My eternal gratitude also goes out to:
Jake Lingwood, for putting up with my deadline surfing during what have been the strangest, but best few months of my life. To Leah Riches for showing me the Polaroids, giving me the gossip and for still coming up with stories, even after the book had been completed. To Chris Sharpe at XL for all of those favours you sorted for me – you're a star. To Mike Champion and Stuart Bishop at Midi Management for their help, and for realizing that a certain crisis was more of a drama than anything else. To John Fairs – more than just a tour manager. Thanks for sorting out the laminates! To James Hyman at MTV, the most enthusiastic librarian ever! Many thanks for the ideas, the chats and, of course, the old magazines. As ever, your input has been competely invaluable – I owe you a huge drink. To Pat Pope, the happy snapper with a dog yapping at his ankles; many thanks for the stories and the photos. To all of the other photographers whose work is featured in this book. To Emma Davis for her interest; sorry, something came up, but many thanks anyway. To Ewen McLeod for the great T in the Park stories. Next time we'll have that drink, mate. To Carol Clerk at the *Melody Maker* newsdesk for the quickest news in town, and for support in the weeks leading up to the happy event! To Victoria Segal for the Dave Grohl stuff,

and Angus Batey for the great article, for introducing Liam to Kool Keith so he could write the amazing 'Diesel Power', and for being a member of the faithful – Toon Army! To Tim Barr the Super Sub and everyone at *Melody Maker* for your ideas and support. And a huge thanks to everyone who contributed to this book through the constant informal chats and also to all of the people who wrote to me from all over the world with your feelings on the band. The Voodoo crew!

Also a huge thanks to my family and friends for their endless support and encouragement.

And finally to Lisa Jayne, my eternal love and thanks for always being there whenever I need you – always. And also for putting up with the mess, the chaos, the stress and the endless promises that I would get the flat sorted – the book's finished now, I'll do the flat tomorrow. But above all, thank you with all my heart and soul for Ruby Blue, our beautiful baby daughter. Born on 17 June, in the middle of the madness; she truly is the last word. Perfect.

Martin James, 1997

Eighty thousand words? I'm not sure I even know eighty thousand words.

Keith Flint, August 1997

Contents

Introduction

The helicopter blades sing like a flanged and chattering pulse in the unseasonably high winds. Below, the classic patchwork quilt of the English countryside stretches into the distance. Above, a blanket of cloud unfolds its oppressive presence, suffocating the sun's attempts to send its rays to the earth below. The atmosphere inside is a mixture of tension, energy and excitement as the chopper's occupants discuss plots, plans and theories; reliving favourite scenes from *Apocalypse Now*.

In the distance a patch of flat farmland has its greenery punctuated by a black and white image; a huge white army ant in full silhouette marked out by a circle of black. The pilot brings the helicopter shuddering towards the ant-like helipad, winds swinging the craft from left to right as nervous tension replaces the previous excitement. As adventures go, this is already an epic.

But this is far more than an adventure. These passengers are on a mission; a brilliantly orchestrated and finely timed mission. From the second they boarded the helicopter the motley collective became part of a greater machine. One whose cogs and wheels rotate through many corners of life. Spreading their mechanical operations across the globe, infiltrating all sections of the media, rolling through the world of publishing, tickling the underbelly of commerce. This is the machine known as the music industry and on this day all eyes and thoughts are focused on a group of hand-picked guests, sent on *this* mission, *this* mad adventure – to attend the first playback of The Prodigy's third and most eagerly anticipated album to date, *The Fat of the Land*. An album which in the coming weeks would crash straight into the number one slots in twenty-three countries, including Britain and America. An album which would become the fastest-selling L.P. of all time, beating both Michael

Jackson's *Thriller* and Oasis's *(What's the Story) Morning Glory?* hands down with sales in excess of three million worldwide, achieved within twenty-four hours of it hitting the record stores.

As the entourage walk into the fourteenth-century barn they are greeted with the sight of a huge PA system and an entirely redesigned interior, complete with fluffy sofas and, more importantly, a bar stacked to capacity with lager; Prodigy lager bearing the same ant logo as the helipad.

'If you see Keith or Liam grab them, take them outside for a quick shoot and then I'll follow to get some quotes,' whispers one journalist to his snapper companion, keen to get one over on the other hacks. 'You'll have to be quick though!'

The invited audience take their places on the fluffy sofas and a flat-capped farmer walks forward with a prize bull in tow. The guest of honour holds its head down, huge horns hinting at its terrifying, violent force, before being escorted out of the barn.

Confusion turns to amusement as the guests joke about the bull's apparent likeness to Keith Flint. Perhaps it's a pantomime bull and the band will emerge in a moment. The atmosphere is relaxed and jovial, and eased by taking huge swigs on the Prodigy branded lager.

Suddenly the conversation is broken by the sound of a huge and funky breakbeat charging from the PA system with more power than a stampeding herd of bulls. 'Smack My Bitch Up' erupts across the barn, stopping people in their tracks. People gasp with amazement before their faces crack into huge smiles. Everyone has known this track for about a year and a half thanks to its regular inclusion in the band's live sets, but to hear it in its full-throttle, perfectly recorded glory is something else entirely. As the album unravels before them, both industry and media know they are hearing history in the making. People grin with astonishment as a unanimous decision is made without a single word being spoken. This is going to be huge.

In the end none of the band bother to show. It's not really their scene.

'All right mate, it's Liam.'

The following day Liam calls me for a quick chat. He isn't particularly bothered by all the fuss about the playback. He knows people are already talking about it but he can't allow himself to be distracted – he's got an album to finish.

'I'm not all that interested in that industry bollocks,' he says over a crackling phone line. 'I heard it went well but I couldn't be bothered to go to it. I was working on the last track to go on the album.'

Eighteen months late, two days before The Prodigy are due to head off on their MTV-conquering tour of the USA and Liam still hasn't finished work on his latest opus. It's typical really. After all, Liam Howlett is a perfectionist who constantly aims to improve upon his own unique songwriting formula. A man at the helm of the most vibrant live band in the world. A band whose legendary shows display a fierce collision between Liam Howlett's bruising, brooding and booming crash sonics, Maxim Reality's confrontational MC-ing and lizard-king antics, Keith Flint's incendiary rabble rousing and, of course, Leeroy Thornhill's high-speed fancy footwork. An act who are as intense as they are unforgettable.

Thanks to the rigours of touring and Liam's unwillingness to release anything but his very best, the version of *The Fat of the Land* that was played in that barn wasn't completed. He was yet to finish 'Serial Thrilla', a new Keith Flint track; the world would have to wait another six weeks to hear it. But hell, the album was eighteen months overdue anyway, so what was another six weeks?

This is the story of those six weeks. And the six years before that. And the madness that followed the album's eventual release on 24 June 1997. It's the story of four reluctant stars coming to terms with an almost overwhelming public profile, while trying to remain true to their underground beliefs. It's a tale of personalities meshing together to create one single united force and of the effects of constant media attention on individual personalities. It's about the thrill-seeking, high-speed motorbike runs, the parachute jumps and the snowboarding sessions. The plane flying, the fast cars and the buzz – always the buzz. The buzz the fans feel, the buzz the band creates, the buzz The Prodigy thrive upon. But above all this is the story of the music and the many adventures that go into it, surround it and help to create it.

Welcome to the world of the Voodoo Crew.

ONE
Everybody in the Place

Sometimes it surprises me that the band came together at all. I'm quite difficult to get on with, I seem quite moody and I don't allow people to come into my space. I was really surprised how quickly me, Keith and Leeroy became like mates who'd known each other for years. Then it was the same with Maxim, like there was a chemistry there. They're fucking cool guys. Really mellow. I couldn't even imagine not being in The Prodigy now.

Liam, August 1997

Deep in the Essex countryside, somewhere between Chelmsford and Braintree, a van pulls up alongside a railway bridge, the side door flings open and a group of friends spill out into the afternoon sun. From the van the soundsystem belts out the latest hip hop mix tape, put together by one of the gang. Public Enemy and Ultramagnetic MCs send their sonic boom beats echoing around the railway bridges as the lads grab their bags. Climbing up the bank they make their way to a huge stretch of bridge wall. This isn't just an ordinary wall though. It's a gallery for the graffiti writers of Essex to show off their talents with a spray can.

Bandanas over mouths and noses, the lads open their bags to reveal an array of spray cans. They've got one thing on their minds; an afternoon of serious bombing. A fevered attempt to claim a stretch of this wall for themselves and make clear their visual presence with a series of multi-coloured markings.

Among them, one lad's work stands head and shoulders above the others. His talent is obvious, his natural ability allows him to take the techniques of graffiti and add immense original flair. His wild-style work spreads across the walls, fluid, vibrant and filled to the last stroke with energy.

As he finishes he stands up and takes a step back to admire the graffiti. He takes off his bandana to reveal a boyish face, skinny with finely marked features. His chin is square and cheek-bones bold, his skin is lightly peppered with a rash of teenage spots. Leaning forward he pulls out another can to add the finishing touches, his tag – FAME.

At the time that tag may have been little more than an adolescent boast in keeping with the arrogance of hip hop's B-boy style, but almost ten years later it seems strangely prophetic. FAME was known to his friends as Liam Howlett, a youth whose path of destiny was soon to take him to the doors of fame, as the musical backbone and spiritual leader of one of the biggest acts on the planet – The Prodigy. Not that he knew it back then. In those days he lived and breathed B-boy culture.

For Liam Paris Howlett, music was almost unavoidable as he grew up in the leafy town of Braintree, Essex. Not that he was force-fed his parent's record collections. Nor did he have an older sibling who would take it upon themselves to educate the younger Liam into the finer nuances of cool. For Liam, discovering the world of music manifested itself in weekly sessions of learning to read music, practising scales and extending his thumb and little finger to reach a full octave on a keyboard. Like so many other kids in the affluent home counties, Liam was, from the age of six, encouraged to indulge in the weekly torture of piano lessons.

At first it meant nothing to him. He was a quiet boy with a manner that was sometimes mistaken for sulkiness, and at that age, learning piano was just another thing that you did as a part of life. However, as he got older the lessons became increasingly awkward. They got in the way of his social life, interrupted BMX sessions with his mates and stopped him from kicking about on his skateboard. But where most kids would simply rebel, Liam had a slight problem – he was good. *Really* good.

His teacher had high hopes for him and this created another problem. In order to reach the goals she had in mind for him, Liam needed to spend time learning to read music. On the other hand, Liam had entirely different ideas. Not only had he developed an outstanding ability on the ivories but he had also discovered a natural talent for memorizing the most difficult pieces. A couple of runs through would be enough for him to learn the piece off by heart, in preparation for the next lesson.

The teacher's excitement at her pupil's musical prowess would soon turn to annoyance as she took the sheet music away from the young piano player and he would continue to play as if nothing had changed.

Soon this weekly battle of wills became something of a trial for Liam and at the age of thirteen the call of his mates became too much. He quit piano lessons.

'I'd have to go while my mates were in the park and things,' recalls Liam. 'In the end I just said to my dad, "I don't wanna do it any more." And he was like, "All right, do what you want." Really mellow and that. My piano teacher was something else though, she started crying when I said I was packing it in. She was going, "No you can't leave. You're really good." But I'd had enough by then. I knew I could play, but what was the point of reading the sheet music?'

So Liam never learned to read those black dots, lines and squiggles. But he'd learned something even more valuable: a natural affinity for music.

When Liam was twelve years old his mother and father split up. Unusually, both Liam and his sister, Natalie, were allowed to stay with their father in Braintree. It was to prove to be an important life change for Liam who was subsequently encouraged by his father to explore all of his creative talents. Liam's growing interest in the world of pop music was supported and encouraged. It was Liam's dad who brought home his first album, *Ska's Greatest Hits* after Howlett Junior had heard bands like The Specials and Madness round at his friends' houses. Meanwhile Liam's already substantial ability for painting and drawing were also coming to the fore.

'I would always sit at home at night watching telly and drawing; used to draw me dad. I did it really well, really realistic. Then I'd I give it to me nan for Christmas and she put it on her wall.'

With his interest growing in both music and art, Liam was almost certainly on course for a creative career. However, with his entry into the local comprehensive school, his path was primed to collide head-on with hip hop culture. It only took one record for Liam to realize this. From the moment that he first heard 'Adventures of Flash on the Wheels of Steel' by the New York rapper Grandmaster Flash, he was hooked.

'It was such a raw record,' he recalls, 'and there was all this other stuff that seemed mixed into Grandmaster Flash; like breakdancing and that. My mate's brother was a DJ and he had this scratching deck. I would just sit in his room listening to these tunes and stuff, I must have been about thirteen. Then that film *Beat Street* came out and I like really got into the whole culture, you know, the hip hop thing. So it was like, going from listening to records in this guy's room and then realizing the whole thing about hip hop wasn't just the music, it was the culture as well. It seemed really touchable, unlike a band on stage; seeing a DJ up there scratching, it was like, "I could learn how to do that." And it was from the street, so there were a lot of people around who were really good breakers and I started to learn breakdancing from them.'

Like many other kids at the time, Liam and his mates would challenge others to breakdancing battles. Unlike others, however, his love of breaking extended to full-on visits to shopping malls to show off his skills. Moving from region to region, throwing down challenges to local breakdance posses for head-spinning battles in the glare of the public eye, out on their Saturday afternoon shopping trips. Inevitably Liam and friends became something of a notorious attraction in the Essex shopping centres in the early 1980s.

Back in the solitude of his house Liam had developed something of a unique graffiti-writing style. His nights of drawing his dad had turned into sessions learning as much as he could about writers like Future 2000, a legend in hip hop circles. As much a part of the scene as the breakdancing and the music, graffiti came naturally to Liam. Not that he was in a hurry to turn his writing skills on the inhabitants, or rather, walls of Braintree. Instead Liam looked to his jacket as a natural canvas for personal expression. The resulting graffitied jacket subsequently became Liam's trademark; a style which friends and neighbours would instantly associate with him. It was also to bring Liam deep into the world of graffiti he'd admired and paid respect to with his own home-bound writing.

While waiting for his train at London's Liverpool Street station, returning home from a breakdancing show at Covent Garden, Liam and his friends were approached by a group of lads from Chelmsford. Coming from this large town about twenty miles from Braintree, the Chelmsford lads had long been feared in neighbouring towns. Long-running feuds existed between the Essex towns of that region, so when this group of Chelmsford boys approached, Liam felt sure that trouble would ensue. To his surprise they simply said something about his jacket and asked if he was into writing.

'I said no, not really,' explains Liam. 'Then we were on the train, and about three stops before Chelmsford they pulled out these markers and destroyed the whole of the carriage. Me and my mate joined in and we completely fucked the train. So after that we all kept on meeting up and kind of formed this graffiti posse. On that line there were loads of bridges and stuff and we used to go there mainly every weekend, during the day because the bridges were mainly in the country. There was one stretch which was about one hundred foot long, it was like a big gallery. I got really into the graffiti side, but eventually, after a few warnings, and after a few friends got into trouble for doing it, I stopped. I stayed on at school, I wanted to get into graphic design and go to art school so I was always pushing my art, not just with the graffiti and stuff. I stayed on to the sixth form when I really changed. I just thought "if I spent a year doing this properly I could get into art college", and that's what I wanted to do.'

Unfortunately it wasn't to be. When he was invited to show his work in an interview at the local art college Liam was confident that a place was inevitably his. After all, he'd finished his qualifications in half the time that it took the rest of his class mates. Added to that, Liam felt, or rather *knew*, that he was *very* good.

'I didn't get in, although my portfolio of my work was much better than the other people – I know because I asked to have a look when we were in the waiting room. I went back and said to the people that were interviewing me, "I know I'm good at this shit, so where's me place?" They said my work was good but there wasn't enough variation in there. So I thought that was that. It just wasn't meant to happen. About a week later though I got a job in London as an art junior at this magazine, which is really what I would have gone for if I'd gone to college for two years anyway. So I missed that two-year college thing, which is cool, and went to work straight away in London for a magazine called *Metropolitan*. I just thought "hah, fuck you" about those poxy college lecturers. I'd proved them wrong, done it without 'em.'

Throughout his years of immersion in the hip hop stylings of breakdancing and graffiti, Liam had also been perfecting another art, one which was to take him to a much higher level of notoriety; DJ scratch mixing. Ever since that first time he'd heard Grandmaster Flash at his friend's house, and then heard his mate's brother scratching on the decks, Liam had been obsessed with the art of the hip hop DJ. Whilst most of his contemporaries had turned into rappers overnight, Liam had set his sights on the science behind the lyrics. Every weekend he would buy records and take them to practise mixing on his mate's decks.

In the summer of 1986, Liam took a job on a local building site to get together the money for his own turntables. It was a gruelling few weeks which saw Liam struggling to keep up with his work mates, his skinny frame aching under the sheer strain of the labour. But it was all worth it in the end. With the money finally saved he bought his own decks and, in typically obsessive style, took to the task of perfecting his scratching, spin-backs and cuts. Within weeks he'd approached Braintree's premier hip hop outfit, Cut to Kill, with a view to DJ-ing for them.

'They were like, "We've already got a DJ but we'll try you out." But I had this attitude that they needed me. I knew I was better than their DJ anyway so they'd have been stupid to turn me down.'

It was a marriage that was to last two years, during which Liam built himself something of a reputation for being a master of the decks. In fact, in 1987 he managed to take both first and third prizes in a radio mixing competition. No mean feat considering that this was on Mark Allen's Capital Radio Show, London's most popular hip hop programme of the time.

'I was always listening to Mark Allen's hip hop show – every weekend,' laughs Liam. 'He used to have like, a mix competition and I entered one mix as DJ Fame, which I thought was pretty good. About a week later I was listening to the tape again and thought "I can do better than that". So I entered something else under a different name, DJ Juice I think it was. Anyway I really scratched it up, totally went for it, so the tapes were like a mile apart from each other. Then a few weeks later I was listening to the show and Mark Allen says, "We've got the winners. second . . . " I don't know, I can't remember now. Anyway next he says my other DJ name and he's going like, "Respect to Braintree" and all that. I couldn't believe it that I came first and third. I never actually told him the truth.'

Despite Liam's commitment to Cut to Kill he continued to hang around with his Chelmsford graffiti mates. They were a pretty tight group of friends by then and spent much of their time going to hip hop events like UK Threshold and UK Fresh (seminal London hip hop jams). Liam was soon to discover that the scene he'd been so enthralled by for the last couple of years had become increasingly gang-centred. In a strange emulation of the US hip hop gang wars eulogized by the gangsta rappers like Ice T and NWA, the UK crews had taken on an almost comically territorial slant. The atmosphere had changed from the collective unity of the people into hip hop, to an oppressive, heavy vibe drenched in bad attitude. The scene was starting to stink.

One night Liam and the Chelmsford boys ventured way outside of their local hood to a hip hop jam in Swiss Cottage, north London. They'd gone down at the invitation of MC Model (who was performing alongside his partner DJ Fingers) who Liam had met a week earlier. As suspicious looks were thrown at them, the group of Essex boys soon felt out of place in the venue. The atmosphere was openly aggressive toward them but they decided to try and ride the storm, deciding that the locals were probably just trying to psych these outsiders out a little. However when MC Model shouted out a "respect to the Chelmsford massive", all eyes were suddenly on Liam's crew.

'I was like, "Fucking hell this is getting a bit dodgy." Suddenly this big black dude pushed us out the back and said, "Give us your money." He gives us loads of this shit, pushing us around and that. They'd got knives and shit and for me it was the end. So we get out of the club and run back to our car – it was a gold Cortina – and my mate's got this fucking gun that he's bought on the black market. I'm going, "What do you think you're doing with that?" He says he's going to settle the score. I couldn't believe it man, it was all too unreal. Like this wasn't what it was about for me. So he slowed the car down just outside the club door, pulled out the gun and just aimed it at this bloke – it probably wasn't even the same one but my mate didn't care – and the guys by the door just froze; stared at the gun and that. And then he just put his foot down and sped off laughing about how he'd showed 'em. I tell you, that whole thing's bothered me for years, man.'

The incident marked the end of Liam's dreams of making it in the hip hop scene. Suddenly he realized that he and his mates would never be accepted and as for Cut to Kill, what could he do? He still loved DJ-ing with the band, still loved the gigs, still loved that special buzz of being part of a creative machine. What Cut to Kill needed was to put out some of their material and try and transcend the posse-to-posse gang bullshit.

One day in early 1988 Liam went in to his job at the magazine as usual. But there was to be nothing normal about this day at all. Thanks to Liam's endless stories about his band, the company's art director had become so enthused that he had decided to invest £4,000 in recording Cut to Kill and putting out an album.

'We basically spent the whole four grand on recording – I think we got slightly ripped off by the guy who was doing it,' Liam recalls. 'We basically spent a day recording it. We ended up with about twelve tracks or something, but didn't save enough cash to do the artwork and promotion. It was stupid, but we were young. We sent out a few white labels to hip hop labels, but I just knew nothing would come out of it."

Soon after this recording Liam left Cut to Kill. He'd grown tired of the hip hop scene; the music wasn't enthusing him in the same way any more and besides, working in London had opened his ears to new forms of music that were filtering through. Every day he would listen to the pirate radio stations blasting out acid-house tracks and some breakbeat-based house tunes. The former left him cold, but the latter got him well and truly fired up.

'It was like hip-hop but slightly faster,' explains Liam who soon bought a keyboard to experiment on some of those sounds he'd been hearing. But there was still something missing; that scene vibe, that togetherness, the entire culture which had first enticed him into hip hop. All this would change on the first night he went to a rave in The Barn, a venue in Rayne, Essex.

'It was mad. There were all these people that I hadn't seen for ages who I used to go to school with, and they were all wandering around, out of their faces on drugs,' laughs Liam. 'I couldn't immediately understand it but I really liked the energy of it. It was almost like, I don't ever want to go to another hip-hop jam again. I was really excited by the music, the beat and the rawness. And the togetherness was fucking amazing. I'd got so used to attitude from the hip hop people that when I saw this, well I was totally blown away.'

Cut to Kill were to go on to sign a single deal on Tam Tam with a track which Liam believed to be his. But he wasn't bothered. His mind was rampaging with excitement over the new possibilities offered by the free party scene. It was 1989 and Britain was heading out on a mad adventure, 'The Second Summer of Love'.

And Liam was dancing right alongside the twenty-four-hour-party people.

*   *   *   *   *

The Barn, Rayne, July 1989
The air is thick with a heady mix of vanilla-flavoured smoke, fresh sweat and the unmistakable scent of ganja as a thousand ravers lift their hands to the sounds being played by resident DJ, Mr C. The atmosphere is electric as a rush of euphoria rides the wave of a piano break. Everywhere smiling faces look to each other with open, welcoming

expressions. The Ecstasy is good tonight and the whole crowd are on the buzz of a loved-up moment. Hairs raise on the backs of necks as complete strangers massage each other's shoulders, and everywhere bottles of water are passed around like liquid peace pipes.

In the middle of this dance are two lads, high with the adrenalin of it all, rushing with the togetherness and buzzing with the E. One is short, about 5' 8", with long, wavy hair. His face is contorted like that of an athlete on the final straight of the four-hundred metres. His eyes suggest that he's about to get the gold medal; they're alive, sparkling under the venue lights. His dancing style looks to be an exaggerated version of running on the spot. Only it's wilder than that, graceful yet unpredictable, a rough and ready street style which seems to jump with the beats.

Next to him dances a tall guy. Impossibly tall, like a basketball player only taller. His black skin is of a light shade, his eyes are warm and friendly and his smile is completely infectious. He lifts his legs as the beats surge in and suddenly he turns into James Brown on amphetamine. His footwork has the complexity of a Northern Soul sequence, seemingly tying and then untying knots in his legs, twisting to the grooves of the hardest house sounds.

Together the duo make a magnetic alliance. Wherever they dance people want to be next to them; their natural charisma, enthusiastic dancing and natural love of the buzz turning them into ambassadors of the having-it-large generation.

The dancers' names are Keith Flint and Leeroy Thornhill. They have only just met, but they will soon start a journey which will see them dancing their way into the history books – soon they will become The Prodigy dancers.

* * * * *

Keith's just so unpredictable but because I know him so well I know how to handle him. He's the mellowest person I know but he's also the most intense person at the same time. One minute he'll be like so laid back, gentle even, and then he's really intense. But it's not really mood swings. It's just like he's both at once – all or nothing.

Liam, August 1997

'You starting something?'

Fighting talk was nothing new to Keith Flint. Not the fighting talk of the hooligan out for a fight on a Saturday night however, but that of someone wired on life, addicted to the experience – and hanging around with the local bad lads to get the right kind of fix.

To Keith, school life was an endless chore, pure and simple. Sitting at the back of the classroom he would stare out of the window, make sarcastic comments or generally mess around, anything rather than actually listen to what the teacher had to say. It wasn't that he lacked intelligence; on the contrary, if the sharpness of his comments were anything to go by, Keith Flint had a very quick mind. But he was easily bored, and school did nothing to stimulate his imagination.

What did turn him on however was hanging around with a group of friends, messing around on the street corners of Braintree, looking for mischief with a never-ending and insatiable thirst for the buzz. School teachers might have described him as disruptive, psychologists might have called him dysfunctional, but his friends called him a good laugh, and this small, occasionally unsure guy was soon considered to be one of the faces around town.

It was little surprise that when it came to school exams Keith failed spectacularly, much to the embarrassment of his mum, who was a school secretary at the time, and his dad, who worked as a civil servant. Keith wasn't bothered though; he wanted a life beyond the rules and regulations of school, beyond the pressures of homework and exams. Although he wasn't quite sure what that was going to be yet.

As soon as he left school he landed gainful employment as an odd-job man, which led on to a succession of jobs. Keith was unable to maintain his interest level to remain in work for any lengthy period of time, but there was something he did love about work – the money.

He was sixteen, the first among his mates to get a job and as such he was the first with any cash at his disposal. As a result he got heavily into buying clothes. But not just any clothes, he was after the expensive designer gear that the casuals wore. In many ways, the casuals represented an extension of the mod ethic of working hard all week to earn enough money for good clothes and a couple of good nights out over the weekend. It was a scene involving a true gang mentality of lads together, out on the town with one thing in mind – pulling a member of the opposite sex. If this didn't happen there was still the chance to get insanely drunk.

If the casual scene of the 1980s was synonymous with anything else, it was Ford Cortinas, furry dice and soccer – or, more to the point, fighting with the fans of the opposition. Being a casual meant being able to pose and preen in a manner which suggested that you were a millionaire, while drinking and fighting in a way which implied that you were slightly unhinged. And as Keith discovered the world beyond the school gates, it was into the very unreal world of the casuals that he walked. They were the only people who made him feel at home with himself.

By the time Keith was seventeen however a new, far more profound influence was to walk into his life. At this point he didn't really have any burning interest in music apart from owning a few punk records and his interest in home life was negligible. All of this changed when Keith's parents divorced, causing him to immerse himself deeper into the casual lifestyle. Keith's dad soon remarried and Keith suddenly had to get used to a stepmother and, more importantly, a stepbrother called Gary.

Gary was the absolute antithesis to Keith. A laid-back hippy who enjoyed smoking dope, he was totally against posing and listened to music by bands like Pink Floyd. At first Keith was suspicious of Gary. Why should he make any effort to become friends with him? After all Keith was planning to get his own place or move in with some mates soon, so the last thing he needed was a new family.

Gary on the other hand saw something in Keith which had been missed by so many others. Under the brash exterior which Keith liked to present to the world, lay a gentle and extremely warm person.

Gary soon befriended Keith and started to introduce him to his alternative lifestyle. They sat up for hours, smoking dope, talking about the world at large and generally discussing dreams. Gary was a man with a wealth of experience, and, just as importantly to the adolescent Keith, he was a man who owned a motorbike. Keith's eyes were quickly opened to the possibilities which lay in the outside world and to the joy of travelling at incredible speeds on a bike.

Gary had come into Keith's life at an extremely important time in his development. A couple of years later and Keith may have remained an Essex casual for good – the house, car, wife and kids included in the lifestyle package. But Keith was still young and impressionable and all of a sudden he realized that there was so much that he wanted from his life.

At first his new-found interest in the hippy lifestyle involved going to the festivals and hanging out, but the laid-back attitudes of the people who surrounded him jarred with the side of his personality which liked excitement, energy and experience. Sure, he may have found the reggae soundsystems great to dance to, but he needed more.

What Keith needed was a life combining the extreme rush of a powerful motorbike with the total chill of good weed, he needed the real experience of travelling.

Soon after, Keith sold his possessions, packed his bags and went off on an eight-month trip through Europe, the Middle East and North Africa. It was 1988, Keith was nineteen and this new world was an exciting place to be. It was a time of living on his wits, making new friends and avoiding getting ripped off.

At the end of the year Keith returned to Braintree, his head full of exciting travellers' tales, eager to take some time out, earn a bit more money, and get back to the travels. Unfortunately his dad had other ideas and Keith was shown the door of the house, his one bag thrown out after him. He had no other choice but to look up old friends for a place to stay. As luck would have it there was a room going in an old house in the town centre. It was a big place which seemed more like a commune. The people in it were really friendly and laid back, and Keith was surprised at how comfortable he felt among them. When one of them suggested that he join them down The Barn for a party, he shrugged his shoulders and went along.

Keith's experiences of nightclubbing were still completely based around his days as a casual. It wasn't a path he particularly wanted to go down again, he wasn't into designer clothes and drinking loads any more. He'd prefer a good smoke and an interesting conversation, followed by a quick jaunt through the leafy streets of Braintree on his bike, which had been stored at a mate's house during his travels. So it was with mild trepidation that Keith, dressed in combats and an Afghan body warmer, went to The Barn.

Within ten minutes of being there Keith Flint was hooked. It was the country's Second Summer of Love and Keith was immediately drawn to the positive vibes, the Ecstasy and the sense of 'up-for-it' energy that seemed to pervade. On any one night it was impossible to tell where things would lead. He might start off at The Barn, or in London at The Astoria, but by the time the sun came up again he could be dancing in a field in the countryside, in a warehouse in London's East End, by the sea in Essex or even in the hippies' place near Braintree. It was exactly the kind of life Keith had been looking for.

It was during these early days of raving that Keith met two people who were to become huge friends. Sharkey was a girl who he'd bumped into at The Astoria and with whom he had struck up an immediate bond. They had a similar attitude, they danced in the same way, and they vibed off each other incredibly. Unlike most of the girls at the time Sharkey really rocked when she danced, she was completely, one hundred per cent into the experience of dancing. Also on that wavelength was the second influential person that Keith met; a cool geezer with all of the right moves – Leeroy Thornhill.

* * * * *

Leeroy's kind of like the mum. He's the guy who sorts out the problems. He's really calm, laid back you know. And if there's a problem he just looks at it and goes, 'OK, I'm going to sort it'. He's a really steadying person to be around.

Liam

Leeroy Thornhill was was born in 1969 in Barking, Essex, but moved to Braintree when he was about three years old. As a child he was an average all-rounder who had a particular passion for sports. In fact he was very good, especially at soccer (to this day he supports Arsenal). To see him play for his school team at the age of eleven may have just given a clue as to Leeroy's next passion – dancing.

For him, music was never far from earshot. One or other of his two elder sisters was always belting out punk records from her room and, inevitably, his sisters were a massive influence on the young Leeroy. At the tender age of ten he found himself hanging around Braintree with the punks and listening to bands like Crass, The Slits, early Clash and even *Dirk Wears White Sox*, the first album from future New Romantics, Adam and the Ants. With this kind of background it was hardly surprising that the first record he bought was by poppy punk band The Boomtown Rats. It was called 'Rat Trap' and it started an obsession in Leeroy which would never die – music.

A few years later, as he discovered his own style, the electro boom happened and Leeroy found himself in the perfect place at the perfect time to soak up a few of the vibes. The youth of the time were buzzing to a trio of films – *Beatstreet*, *Breakdance* and *Wildstyle* – and Leeroy was instantly impressed enough to immerse himself in certain aspects of B-boy culture. Whilst this didn't extend to graffiti, it did include the more energetic breakdancing, with the lanky Leeroy practising his aerials, windmills and headspins every night after school. When he wasn't bombing around town on his BMX that was.

As he got older, this love of electro and subsequently hip hop became increasingly refined and Leeroy found himself getting deeply into funk and rare groove. He was sixteen and already he had developed a strong fascination with James Brown, or more to the point, the great man's dancing style.

'James Brown is your man of course,' enthuses Leeroy. 'If there's anyone I look up to, it's him. Some of the things he does, the slides and the way his feet move, are just superb.'

There was also another influence on Leeroy's dancing style: not as famous as James Brown but just as important to Leeroy, a mate of his called Paul Jones.

'He was just such a great dancer, I used to watch him to learn a few steps. Not that I ripped him off but he was just excellent to watch.' With Jones and the rest of their mates, Leeroy would head off to the rare groove parties in London which dominated the dance underground scene until 1987. The crew soon gained considerable notoriety for their dancing and they quickly found that there were bonuses to being great dancers.

'It was like everybody would want to dance with us, man. And there would be loads of girls too.'

It was a lifestyle which was to take him all around the home counties, living for the groove, dancing until his feet were sore. Then, at the age of eighteen Leeroy was to make a decision which would bring his days of rare groove partying to a temporary halt – he took a job as an electrician in Bath. Two hundred miles away from his home town and in an area where rare groove and funk just wasn't so popular.

Leeroy started working seven-day weeks so that he could take occasional long weekends in order to go back to Braintree and the clubs he loved. It was while he was working in Bath that his mates started telling him about the free party scene. They were constantly enthusing about The Barn and about the acid house that was being played there. Leeroy had heard this acid house stuff and, to be frank, he hated it. He thought it was soulless: it lacked funk, groove, any of the ingredients that made him want to slide and shuffle his feet.

'People I knew in Bath kept on saying that I should go to some of their local events,' Leeroy recalls. 'These parties with three thousand people dancing, with an amazing atmosphere. It sounded good but I just kept on thinking "no, it's not really for me. I won't like it". So I never went.'

It's ironic that here was a man who lived to dance and the first-ever entirely dance-based sub-cultural explosion didn't seem to be his thing. Like an ostrich with his head firmly planted in the sand, Leeroy steadfastly refused to check out the raves.

One weekend back in Braintree, however, he finally agreed to go to The Barn; as much to keep his mates from going on at him as anything else.

'I got in there and I was like trying to dance to this music and I felt nothing at all. It was all too fast, just no funk at all. It just seemed so repetitive and dull, like constant bleeps and stuff. And then I had an E; my first one. I just necked it and it all started to make sense.'

Leeroy's senses were suddenly alive to the sounds – the sub bass, the strange frequencies and the odd filtering. And the beats suddenly came alive too, opening a door for him to convert his James Brown stepping to the acid house groove. A dancing style which was so different from the rest of the clubbers' moves that he proved an irresistible force. All night people came up to him. He made loads of new friends and together they all danced until the club shut, after which they went on somewhere else and danced some more.

Leeroy was hooked and the following day he talked incessantly about what had happened. Like so many others of his generation he'd had a life-changing experience which seemed to him on an almost biblical level. He knew he had to be a part of this scene so, for the next nine months, he divided his time between Bath and Braintree, working as hard as he could to earn the money to get home for a solid bout of raving.

It was during this time that he hooked up with Keith. The two of them instantly attracted by each other's dance style. Together they travelled all over the place, chasing the party scene. A journey which would eventually lead them to Liam Howlett.

* * * * *

Maxim's just so laid back, really cool you know. But when he gets on stage it's like he gets this completely different personality. But the

**rest of the time he's just so chilled . . . until he gets a drink inside him
–then God help all of us.**

Leeroy

Peterborough. A large town or a small city depending on your point of
view. A place you travel through on the train to the north-east of
England. The passport centre for the south-east of England. And that's
about it. Nothing to get excited about really. Except for one thing – its
music scene.

Peterborough was a punk haven from 1977, a centre for two-tone in
1979 and a reggae stronghold throughout the 1980s. Whatever the
reason, whether it was because there was nothing much to do, or
because there was a high level of unemployment, Peterborough has long
boasted a strong musical community.

It was into the Peterborough reggae soundsystem scene that a young
Keith Palmer was introduced by his brother, Starkey Ban Tan, ten years
Keith's senior and one of four brothers and sisters. Nicknamed Keeti by
his friends Keith had previously been a huge two-tone fan. ('The Specials
remind me of The Prodigy because they were like a gang, completely
untouchable.') Once introduced to the soundsystem vibe however he
instantly connected on a creative level and he soon took up the
microphone, started chatting and slowly built up a reputation for his
fast-style licks. His brother, to this day an acclaimed MC on the reggae
scene, pushed Keith to the forefront, even encouraging the youngster to
drop his own name in favour of the much sharper Maxim Reality.

Maxim was seventeen when he played his first gig at a club in
Basingstoke. It was an experience which gave him a taste for
performance which he'd never lose. It also encouraged him to start
playing his own music. A few months later he sent off for a list of
musicians looking for vocalists which the Musicians' Union was
circulating. It was through this list that he hooked up with Nottingham
producer Ian Sherwood, aka Sheik Yan Groove.

The deal was simple: Ian would supply the music and Maxim would
come up with lyrics. The set up was very basic, put together by Ian from
his earnings at the local prison, but what he produced was interesting
enough for Maxim to record a few tracks.

'Basically what he was doing was that Go-Go stuff with a shuffle
beat,' explains Maxim. 'It was jack music, which wasn't really my thing
but it did open me up to different music.'

Indeed it was through Ian that Maxim discovered the delights of George Clinton's incarnations as Parliament and Funkadelic. Nottingham had an extremely strong funk and rare groove scene with its top nightclub, Rock City, gaining a huge reputation for its superb rare groove all-dayer to which Maxim was a regular visitor.

Unfortunately the pairing with Sheik Yan Groove proved to be unfruitful in the search for a recording contract and Maxim headed off on a brief travelling stint across Europe and North Africa.

'When I came back I was faced with the choice of "do I move to London or do I stay in Peterborough for the rest of my life?" In the end I chose London because two of my friends moved there and nothing was doing for me at home.'

Once in London Maxim became heavily involved in the capital's soundsystem scene, while also soaking up the influences from the hip hop scene. Yet the rave scene just left him feeling cold.

'I did go to a couple of raves before The Prodigy but I wasn't into it. The thing is I was into the funk stuff and hip hop. I loved the reggae stuff but I'd also listen to rare groove. I mean I was into the dance scene before rave even happened, the Caister Weekenders and that, so when acid started coming in, and it was all just bleeping and burping, I wasn't into it. The thing is I only ever smoked weed, I never did any chemicals so I couldn't get on that vibe. I just used to say, "I don't do man-made drugs man".'

So, when Ziggy, an old mate of Maxim's from Peterborough, called him to say he knew of a rave band who were looking for an MC, Maxim wasn't exactly bowled over with joy. But at the same time he was always looking for new styles of music to explore so he suggested that someone get a tape to him.

'So I sent him a tape, phoned up and I thought for a minute I was going to get attitude, that reggae attitude,' explains Liam. 'And he said, "Yeah man, I really like the tape. It's really different."'

A couple of weeks later Maxim travelled down by bus to meet The Prodigy. It was 1990 and he and his prospective new band were due to play that night at a grotty rave in the East End of London. Maxim was, to say the least, uninterested. This just wasn't going to be his thing, man; maybe he'd do a couple of gigs for the crack, but that was it. He had his career to think of after all.

* * * * *

For one brief naive moment in the late eighties, in a field off the M25 at an acid house party, or at an urban warehouse party we all believed that things might change. Like our parents did in the sixties. And maybe for a short time things were different.

Sarah Champion, Disco Biscuits

It is difficult to explain the sheer euphoria which surrounded the free party acid house scene from the late 1980s until 1994 when the Criminal Justice Act finally turned the party people into criminals. It was a time of chasing a whisper of a rumour of a party. A time when the sheer vibe of being there, dancing in a field in the middle of the countryside to a soundsystem held together with sticky-backed plastic and spliff ash had an unusual, almost spiritual vibrancy. Everyone seemed to be locked into a unified desire to find the party and feel the beat. Something special seemed to be hanging in the air, a weird and no-doubt wired knowledge which those with an ear to the ground instantly tuned into.

Much of the energy which cloaked these parties was a sense of being turned on to a secret. There was a renegade society which already had its own infrastructure, one so organized that the soundsystems could take a site mid-afternoon, circulate the location along the subterranean grapevine which existed among Britain's increasingly disenfranchized youth by the evening and, come the witching hour of midnight, a field in the middle of nowhere would become dramatically transformed into a dancefloor for a mass of joyous people. While the music business, the media and, realistically, the majority of the nation's youth population scurried around, chasing the latest indie hopefuls, those who were eventually to become known as the ravers were locked into an endless cycle of hard partying – twenty-four hours a day and seven days a week if at all possible. It was, to put it mildly, a special time. And one which has had a profound and lasting effect on British culture.

The free party scene naturally had its critics. People brought up on a staple diet of rock, guitars and superstars, who couldn't understand the primal pleasure in dancing to an endless stream of beats made by a faceless producer, and played by that representative of every naff party that ever happened down the local rugby club, the bloody DJ. These unenlightened onlookers simply put this party-powered energy down to the revolutionary nature of the drug which seemed to be central to things: MDMA, or Ecstasy. A drug which, it was claimed, heightened the sense of togetherness, increased the need to dance. For many, this chemically induced *bonhomie* marked the scene out as being void of any real value, as if having a good time wasn't cerebral enough to have any worth placed upon it.

As the theorists argued over the reasons for the state of bliss which had gripped so many people that it could no longer remain a hushed secret, the ravers just got on with the task in hand. Which invariably was to find the next party. And if that road led to the odd Ecstasy rush along the way, they just went with it, smiley badges pinned to their spirits like shining beacons in a depressing world.

Into this scene walked a skinny youth from Braintree, hair cut into a wedge, or curtains as some called them, dressed to the nines in B-boy cool. A lad who'd become used to nights out involving a certain amount of bad attitude and a whole lot of hassle. Imagine the scene as he first walked in on the party people at The Barn.

Stepping through the door he would have been instantly aware of the boom, boom, boom of the kick drum, the out-of-this-planet acidic noises and the thunder of the gut-churning sub bass. He would have been overcome by the sheer volume of sweaty people dancing like wild things, grinning like maniacs. People who he'd gone to school with and maybe never really got on with would have turned to him and smiled in a welcoming way. This was everyone's party. A space where conflict ceased to matter, attitude was checked into the cloakroom and the bad taste of the world outside was washed down with a gulp of water and a pill. Chances are that the skinny B-boy, the quiet yet confident scratchmaster would have felt both exhilarated and confused. Like an alien discovering that his spiritual home was in fact a few solar systems away from his current place of residence.

The Barn was like nothing Liam Howlett had experienced before but he was uncharacteristically drawn to the vibe. And as the beats washed over him and his feet started to shuffle to the insistent grooves he went with the flow and lost himself to the party fever. It was a complete revelation to him and within an hour he was completely hooked.

'It was really fucking amazing. Also it was the first time I'd ever taken an E. And my mates and me were really buzzing. I don't know. It was something really special. From then on I used to spend all my time during the week looking forward to the weekend because I just loved the buzz so much.'

That first E didn't turn Liam into the gurning idiot that the papers would like to portray E-heads as being. It brought him into the vibe, helped him understand the energy and provided him with an overwhelming sense of belonging. It was more like a warm initiation than a mindless rush into the unknown. Yet, unlike for the majority of the people populating the free party universe, Ecstasy didn't become Liam's recreational drug of choice. No, he preferred something a little more unpredictable.

'I was more into acid really, to be honest. I was really paranoid about Ecstasy,' he says, a grin creeping across his face. 'It was weird because like people were sort of saying they'd got no energy because of the E. So I was more into acid. LSD is much more effective than Ecstasy really . . . so it was kind of nice to do that as a first drug. And I was always smoking but that was normal really. LSD is so out of the normal, you feel completely out of control. It was pretty scary, but I used to just take it and like, try and control it. I remember trying to get back home and there was this three-mile walk. I used to arrive home all covered in dirt. I've got to say it was a fucking adventure. I never knew where I was going to turn up, or even if it was going to be good. It was like a real adventure. That was one of the things I loved about the whole rave thing, the adventure. After we done The Barn, we were always still buzzing on the drugs, so afterwards we used to go down to this beach which was about two miles away. It was summer so you can imagine the vibes; hot summer mornings, the sun rising and a load of people having a good time. It was like way down, a couple of miles from the road, and it was a nudist beach so people would be coming down in the morning to get an all-over tan and all they'd see was a load of ravers dancing, and me DJ-ing out of the back of the van.'

Of course it was completely natural that Liam would instantly dive into DJ-ing at these parties. After all wasn't that exactly what he'd been doing during those years of trying to get accepted into the hip hop scene? There was a difference here though, these people, the so-called ravers, actually appreciated his DJ-ing skills. They got a buzz from his deft mixing, his ability to drop just the right tune to take the mood even higher. And the crowd would let him know that they loved it.

Unlike most of the DJs surrounding Liam, he didn't play sets stuffed to the gills with Chicago house cuts and he definitely avoided the acid house stuff. What he loved were the breakbeat tunes. After all, once a B-boy, always a B-boy. However, along with his love of hip hop, Liam had also developed something of a love for 1970s funk, so for him, if the beat wasn't funky it wasn't worth the vinyl it was pressed on. He quickly gained a reputation for his funked-up breakbeat sets.

'I used to go into record shops and I'd be looking for records for fucking hours; I'd spend hours in there listening to records. I used to listen for the breaks, the ones on the slightly more funkier side, you know,' he recalls. 'It was a bit of a habit really, but I was totally into it. I always knew exactly what kind of stuff I was after and I wouldn't stop until I'd found something that would work. Yeah, it had to be funky with good breakbeats.'

Liam's funked-up DJ-ing sets proved to be an intrinsic presence at the free parties in his corner of Essex. One such post-Barn location was an old house belonging to a hippy who felt that the ravers were somehow spiritually linked to his 'turn on, tune in and drop out' generation. Or maybe it was the drugs he liked. Either way, he let the ravers use the grounds of his house for their parties.

The house lay in a small village, deep in the Essex countryside. A sleepy three-house village which would be transformed into a manic party zone after the clubs had closed. With a soundsystem set up in the house and strobes flashing continuously, the village would rock to the sonic boom of the rave until things gradually dispersed over the next twenty-four hours.

Each week the venue for the free party could change. There was a spur-of-the-moment atmosphere about things; a real sense of living on the edge and going with the flow of events. It was during one of the nudist-beach parties that the first seeds of The Prodigy were sown.

Liam was DJ-ing from the back of the van when a bloke he recognized from Braintree came up to him. He was small, dressed in combats and a sheepskin jacket and he had an intense, yet amiable air about him. Like someone who thrives on meeting new people; someone who loves the buzz of new places, new experiences and new friendships. It was, of course, Keith Flint.

'I met Keith at this party and he came up to me and said, "What's that tune you were playing?" And I was saying how I played more breakbeat-orientated stuff than four-to-the-floor, and you know, just telling him about the kind of tracks I was into. I don't know, we were both off it really, but we kind of connected in some way. But that was a normal thing then.'

Later that night Keith asked Liam if he would do him a tape of his tunes. Again not an unusual thing for the time, as the DJs weren't stars back then and to be able to share the music was as natural as sharing the party experience. So Liam obliged, in fact he probably even made a couple just to make sure that he gave Keith the best possible tape.

However, instead of filling both sides of the tape with his favourite dub plates he decided to stick a few of his own tunes on side two. Just to try them out on someone new – like a private experiment.

'I'd got this keyboard, which was a workstation, so you could basically make a whole piece of music on it. All through, end of 1989 and 1990, I was writing all my own tracks. I wasn't trying to do it to sell, I was doing it for myself, to inspire me, rather than just going down the pub. Then I gave a tape to Mr C who was the resident DJ at The Barn. I was like, "Here's me tape, man, give it a listen will you." And a week later he goes, "Yeah man, listened to the tape. I can get you a record deal on Bad Records." I mean it was this dodgy little label but I was like, "Well do it, do it . . . I'm up for it, man." Nothing ever happened with that. It must have been the drugs talking. Anyway at the same time I was putting all these demos I was making on one side of a tape and a DJ mix on the other. I was doing that for months at a time and it was one of these that I gave to Keith. I remember thinking at the time that the selection of my own tracks and the mix itself were both really strong.'

It was September 1990, Liam had changed jobs and was now working in a T-shirt printing company in Braintree for more money than he'd previously earned. The extra cash was spent on his weekly record-buying habit, and subsequently Liam's on-tape mix selection was a perfect representation of the scene. So when he pulled up his car beside Keith and passed over his tape he felt confident that his new friend would appreciate the vibe.

Keith did more than simply 'appreciate the vibe'. He positively jumped with it the second he slipped it into the car stereo. Keith and Leeroy were on their way home from Raindance, one of the most popular raves in the country at the time. The duo were on a total buzz from their night of dancing among the people they loved; the party people. They needed some music to keep the mood going, and to try and prolong the final effects of the E. Scanning the airwaves in search of a local pirate station the twosome started to despair; they needed sounds and they needed them that minute. Suddenly Keith remembered the tape that Liam had done, which was still in his sheepskin pocket. On one side it said 'MIX', the other simply had the word 'PRODIGY', which Keith faintly remembered Liam saying was his own stuff. So he slipped it into the stereo. The mix side was perfect, blending some of Keith and Leeroy's favourite tunes of the time. It was a selection of the very best of the underground, guaranteed to keep the deepest raver happy. Then Keith turned the tape over . . . and he couldn't believe his ears. The B-side was absolutely brilliant.

A mix of rampant breakbeats and ruffneck techno, Liam's own stuff was a funk-fried trip. Instant, almost commercial, yet undeniably underground, it tapped straight into the vibes of the time and, more importantly, gave clues to the possible future of the ever-changing soundtrack of the scene.

Both Keith and Leeroy were dumbstruck. They just kept rewinding and listening to Liam's tracks all the way home. And when they got home it was straight to the stereo system, tape on, volume up to the max. The duo danced for hours, completely turned on to Liam's hardcore digi-funk, and eventually resolved to approach Liam the next time they saw him, and to make him an offer – to dance on stage with him when he played live.

Liam wasn't so sure to begin with. He did want to play live at some point – he'd loved it back in his Cut to Kill days, but he had never thought about having dancers, let alone these two geezers who he'd only just met.

'Keith was living in this big house in Braintree at the time. It wasn't exactly a squat, more like a rented café, but it was where all of the party people kind of lived really. A really sociable place, we'd all just go there after a night out to chill. It was like everyone at the end of the night would know each other and stuff and that was cool. It was always full of different people just talking to each other, spending time. You know I felt really comfortable there, I never felt embarrassed when I was chatting, which wasn't like me at that time. Keith came up to me one night and says, "I heard your tape and I'd really like to talk to you about doing something with it." It was like . . . well, Keith was such a character, even then. He was such a fucking poser, he used to wear this jacket which was like a sheep – a sheepskin, all fluffy on the outside. He was Mr Raver. He really was. Always wearing army greys and always wearing this sheep. He was such a fucking poser. Anyway he suggests this dancing idea which was a bit of a surprise really. Keith and me, we were like people who'd see each other every now and again in different places, you know, The Astoria in London and that. We weren't mates or anything but most of those places were small and there'd always be a particular crowd who would go down. He used to be with a crowd that I never really knew. And he was a couple of years older than the lot that I knew so I never really knew him. When he'd go into a club and started dancing, people would always come up to him and dance with him. Wherever he went he'd always manage to get people dancing around him. He was quite a man to watch. Very magnetic.'

Keith, on the other hand, was hardly able to contain his excitement about the idea. Imagine it, Liam's tunes, Leeroy and Keith doing what they did best, dancing for the crowds. And then there was Sharkey as well. Had Keith mentioned Sharkey to Liam? Well, she was going to be a part of it as well.

Despite any reservations Liam might have had, he decided to go with it. After all, he had nothing to lose.

'Keith was buzzing about being on stage and saying, "Imagine we could do this", not trying to work out a routine, but just buzzing about it. In the end I just went, "Yeah, let's do it."'

It was that simple really. No advertising for band members in the back pages of *Melody Maker*, no lengthy auditions and certainly no arguments over the name. The Prodigy it was to remain. Liam had chosen the monicker in honour of his Moog Prodigy keyboard. The very piece of equipment which had enabled him to create this musical beast, in his own bedroom.

Liam was part of a quiet revolution going on behind the closed curtains of Britain's bedrooms. All over the country, kids were knocking out tunes with their basic samplers and Atari computers. Home-made, cut-and-paste studios which would have your average studio engineer laughing at the primitive nature of it all, were springing up everywhere. The kids driving these low-budget machines were the very same people who were responsible for the records which were being played at the raves. Recorded at home, pressed up on to a limited run of white labels and then playing out at the nation's biggest raves a few days later. It was all part of the energy, the vibrancy that enabled people to take control of this part of the industry. A side of the music business which had long been out of reach for the kid on the street. Suddenly the kids were drawing up their own rules which excluded the industry's usual business practices and replaced them with the renegade practices of the underground. Just as the parties and raves were being put on by people who'd never promoted a rock gig in their lives but understood what the ravers wanted, so too these young producers ignored the mainstream and went straight for the scene they knew best; the rave scene.

Wherever there is a creative individual there is guaranteed to be a mate who wants to be the manager. Enter Ziggy, a friend of Keith's who knew a lot of the DJs, promoters and label owners.

'Ziggy always used to go to The Barn every week. He was about twenty-nine and a bit of a businessman – into double-glazing so he had a bit of a business head on him. So we let him become our manager. He was useless really.'

Not all *that* useless though. Within a week he'd got The Prodigy their first booking and thanks to one his contacts in Peterborough he was able to access the final brick in The Prodigy wall – an MC. Since Keith had first come up with his plan to take The Prodigy live, Liam had done a bit of planning of his own. A bloke behind a keyboard and three people dancing wasn't, he decided, enough to satisfy a crowd. It wasn't vibrant enough to fully capture people's imaginations so he hit upon the idea of getting an MC to whip up the crowd. After all, a lot of the DJs used them and they were pretty much an intrinsic part of any rave.

Ziggy's MC mate was one Maxim Reality, a stalwart of the reggae scene. His credentials were (on paper at least) a bit of a risk for an up-and-coming rave act, but Liam liked taking risks. He still does today.

'Ziggy just goes to me, "He's a wicked MC and his hair sticks out like this" (making wild gestures with his hands on his head). I just thought, "What the hell, it might work. And if it doesn't he's out."'

In the event Maxim most certainly stayed and The Prodigy was born.

TWO
You Know the Score

It's such a buzz when we're together, better than any drug in the world and nobody can come between us. We're very tight.

Maxim

They had such an energy about them. Every time they played it was like a fuckin' energy man, like the whole rave just lifted to another level. They were like really locked into the spirit of the rave, the buzz. But it was really aggressive as well – in an E-ed-up way, you know? There was an edge. But those costumes man, someone should have told them what they looked like. I mean they looked like jockeys, man. Especially Keith 'cos he's so short anyway! But then again, that's the main thing I can remember from The Labyrinth days now. No details about songs or shit. Just the vibe, and those friggin' costumes.

Andrew Cunningham, East London. Prodigy fan since 1991

It was 1990. The rave parties were still based in warehouses and small clubs in the country's city centres, stretching the venue's capacities weekly and threatening the big outdoor raves that were to follow. Ziggy had only been The Prodigy's unofficial manager for a week when he announced the band's first booking. The impending debut of The Prodigy was to be in Dalston at The Labyrinth. A particularly rough area of London and a club with a reputation for one or two unpleasant dealings. Nonetheless Liam, Keith, Leeroy and Sharkey all headed down to the club in Keith's battered old car. Maxim was to be coming down on his own, having memorized the songs from the tape Liam had sent him. Amazingly this was to be the very first meeting between the Braintree posse and their would-be MC.

Keith's car pulled into Dalston a number of hours before the band were due to perform. Partly due to a rampant attack of nerves, and partly to Liam's need for things to be perfectly in control (some risks were too stupid to take) their arrival at their first ever gig was, to say the least, a little premature. But The Prodigy were, if nothing else, keen to get their first night right.

'Keith parked his car out the back about eight hours before we went up on stage,' laughs Liam. 'I mean it, we were there almost eight hours before we had to be. It was fucking mad but we had quite a lot of people coming down, about thirty from our way, and we wanted things to be perfect. And the guy who run it, Joe, was basically letting us play Friday night – the quiet night. Saturday night was the main night and we wanted him to give us that slot.'

Such was the excitement surrounding the performance that the band decided an image was essential in order that they would stand out visually as well as musically. At the back of Liam's mind was the worry that it might not look powerful enough. A few days before zero-hour Keith phoned Liam to tell him his idea for costumes. The concept: green and white harlequin-style track suits with white and green circles emblazoned on them. They looked faintly ridiculous, but somehow it helped The Prodigy to become firmly placed in the minds of the ravers. But green and white cut-and-paste clothing! What was that all about?

'God knows how we did it, but we got these costumes,' shudders Liam. 'I think basically what happened is Keith started saying, "I'm going to get this green costume made with a circle on it", then, all-of-a-sudden me wanting to do it as well. I was thinking, "Yeah, this is going to be our image." I think it's one of the biggest mistakes I've ever made.'

It is an image which was to haunt them for ever more, with music papers reprinting the photos of them in their stage gear long after they'd dropped the look.

Back then on their first night in Dalston, the newly assembled band were preparing themselves, calming their nerves and sharing banter. The Essex crew met Maxim and they all seemed to get along fine, although it was perhaps difficult to tell with Maxim whose quiet seriousness can be off-putting at first meeting. Maxim, a veteran of the soundsystems, showed few signs of nerves thanks to his comparatively vast experience. In contrast, the others were like kittens in a sack; a bag of nerves in other words. And then, as if things weren't tense enough, the promoter offered them this little gem: The Prodigy were actually only the second act to have played at the venue. The first one apparently got bottled off. The band were terrified. Although, years later, Liam admits that it might just have been a wind up. 'I reckon he just wanted to scare us a bit. You know, have a bit of fun with the Essex boys.'

Eventually the Essex boys (and girl) stepped out on stage to play. The Prodigy ran through a set which lasted for eight songs. Liam pushed his – by today's standards – primitive keyboards, wrapping circuits around tracks which featured on his demo tape. Cuts like 'Android' and 'Everybody in the Place' rumbled into The Labyrinth, flowing like smoke through the PA. Meanwhile, Leeroy shuffled his huge swinging gait through footwork fancier than Pele's, moves that would have brought a smile to James Brown's face, had he been there to see it. Keith worked himself through a series of high-speed, running-on-the-spot styles, grinning at the crowd and encouraging them to feel the vibe, while Sharkey displayed her individual rocking style of dancing. Where most girls at the time were trying to perfect a dirty slow-grind routine, Sharkey's style was full-on and hard. A perfect complement to Keith's, in fact.

'Sharkey was someone Keith and Leeroy had met,' Liam explains. 'She never came to The Barn but she knew 'em from the Astoria. She lived in London and she was always at the best parties. She was like a rapper you know, loads of front. Really charismatic, like Keith. Her and Keith used to get on a buzz and dance together whenever they were out. Not on the stage so much, but on the dancefloor. And then he said to me, "There's this girl Sharkey who wants to get up on stage as well." And I was like, "Well yeah, OK."'

In the end, a crowd of approximately two hundred and fifty punters saw the debut Prodigy gig (although Liam maintains that the number was more like five hundred). Either way it was a resounding success, and a gig which remains clear in Liam's memory: 'I remember being just really, really nervous. It was weird there were a lot of people from home there. We didn't want to make ourselves look knobs in front of them. If we didn't know anyone it didn't matter but in front of our mates . . . it was like, terrifying. I was much quieter them days, just basically keeping myself to myself, so getting up on stage made me really nervous. Seeing me mates just made me shit scared. But then when we first started I was just over the moon. I just wanted to play the music and things went down really well. In fact we rocked it.'

'Rocked it' perhaps, but there were a couple of little problems which needed sorting out. The first one was easy to deal with; cutting out the E on stage. In order to calm down those pre-gig nerves all of the band, barring Maxim, had shared a couple of Es. The result found the dancers, particularly, losing their edge. Becoming lost during various points of the songs. 'I was so over-buzzed I couldn't get into it,' acknowledges Liam. They vowed never to do any drugs before going on stage again, although Liam now admits, 'I think Keith and me probably did it a few more times.' Either way, the negative feelings that they had about their states of mind during that first gig were enough to make them deal with the situation.

The other problem was far more pressing. A musical problem that Liam had to sort out. Maxim's ragga-style delivery didn't sit too well with the sounds that Liam was producing. 'Keeti was rapping over the top of the music and so I was like, saying that's not the vibe. It's more a connection to the crowd.'

In the two weeks before the band's next booking, Liam managed to make Maxim fully aware of what this music required. The rave scene was more about sharing the vibe than talking up an individual. Fortunately Maxim very quickly understood. He'd already learned from that one gig and as soon as Liam put the ideology of The Prodigy into words, Maxim got the full picture.

But there was more to this picture. More even than the rest of the band could have realized. Only a month after that debut gig, Liam had some news which would change The Prodigy for ever. He had secured a record deal with one of Britain's leading house labels – XL Records.

* * * * *

'Yeah, can I speak to Nick Halkes please. Tell him it's Liam Howlett from The Prodigy.'

'Hello, Nick speaking.'

'Yeah Nick. My name's Liam Howlett, I make music as The Prodigy and I was wondering . . . '

' . . . if you could come in and play me some stuff. Well, tell me a little bit more.'

'Well, what I'm doing is kind of like techno but on this B-boy tip. I mix breakbeats with raw techno and it rocks man, you've got to hear it.'

'Yeah OK, that sounds interesting. Can you come in next week?'

'Yeah man, I'll see you then. Cheers.'

Click. Buzz.

'Another bunch of no hopers, no doubt,' shouts a bemused Nick Halkes to the company press officer, Leah Riches. 'I don't know why I bother with these demo meetings.'

To think it could have all been so different. Had Nick Halkes been in a bad mood, perhaps suffering a hangover or post-weekend comedown, then he might just have told Liam to send in the tape, so that it would get added to the inevitable mountain of unsolicited demos. Thankfully Nick had a reputation for being conscientious, so when he heard this quiet, almost monotonal voice on the other end of the phone getting increasingly excited just describing the music he was making, he had to meet up with the guy. It was a meeting which would remain lodged in the memory banks of everyone who was in the office that day.

'I remember this group of lads coming into XL's offices,' recalls Leah Riches who would become The Prodigy's press officer for almost five years. 'There were loads of them all hanging around the foyer while Liam took his tape to play to Nick Halkes. I just kept on thinking "what the fuck is this, who are these people?" I think Keith might have been there, maybe Ziggy, but all I could really see was this mass of lads standing around, looking a bit nervous. When they'd gone Nick came out of his office, smiled at me and said, "I'm signing him." He'd decided there and then, on the spot, which is something I'd never seen him do before. I think it's safe to say that this was the shrewdest A&R decision that Nick ever made.'

Almost a week after that meeting at XL, Liam was back in the daily routine of his job, doubtless dreaming of the weekend ahead. Suddenly the phone rang. It was Nick Halkes for Liam. Halkes announced that XL Records were going to offer The Prodigy a single deal. Liam put the phone down, tried to gain his composure but failed. Within seconds he was jumping around the printing shop, overtaken by pure unadulterated joy.

'It was like the best thing that had ever happened to me. I couldn't believe, I mean I knew that my stuff was good, but I wasn't expecting such a quick reaction from a label. God knows what the people I worked with must have thought, but I went absolutely fucking mad, just punching the air and running around shouting.'

It was surely a sight to savour. This normally quiet lad who would come to work on a Monday morning with huge, dark bags under his eyes and recounting tales of dancing all weekend, dancing around the print workshops like a man possessed.

For Liam, signing to XL had a very sweet taste. Not only had it been one of only two tapes that he'd actually played to any record company (the other going to Tam Tam who had signed Cut to Kill but turned The Prodigy down flat) but it was also a label which had put out some of his favourite records of the time; such as Frankie Bone's seminal 'Bones Breaks'.

The demo which Liam played to Halkes was the very same selection that had been on Keith's tape. It was a rough marriage of techno and breakbeats with edges so sharp it could cut the air. Good enough however for four of the demo tracks to be proposed as the debut single: 'What Evil Lurks', 'We Gonna Rock', 'Android' and 'Everybody in the Place'.

Strangely, news of the imminent single release wasn't greeted with the same excitement by the rest of the troupe. Keith, Leeroy and Sharkey had only ever seen the performances as an extension of raving. An enjoyable addition to the immense buzz they were already on. Putting out a single made things totally different. Suddenly it all seemed a bit too serious.

In fact, prior to approaching Liam with ideas about dancing on stage Keith had already booked a ticket to travel to Thailand and, but for a series of disastrous events, he would have gone through with it. First of all his grandmother died, which resulted in Keith rearranging his departure date so that he could attend her funeral. Then his travel money was stolen and finally, just to top things off, he got arrested for smoking a joint in London's Soho Square. As a result he was forbidden to leave the country prior to his court case. Not that he could afford it any more.

Years later Maxim still looks upon these events as having some mystical power behind them. As if Fate was holding all of the band's cards, pushing them towards their futures in The Prodigy.

'If you think about it, this was meant to happen to us,' he explains. 'I mean, there was nothing to make me come to that first gig, I wasn't even into rave. Then when that deal came along, well, I was still wanting to do my own stuff so I almost left then, but something stopped me. And all that stuff with Keith having his travel plans fucked. Well that's got to be fate. We had no choice man, it was all meant to happen.'

* * * * *

I didn't think about how much I was going to get fucking paid, it was enough of a buzz to have a record coming out on XL. And then when the record came out. I remember being down The Barn and the DJ played it. Everyone was fucking coming up to me you know, like really into it. It was fucking amazing.

Liam

In February 1991, The Prodigy's first EP 'What Evil Lurks' hit the nation's record shops. A rough-around-the-edges marriage of renegade breakbeats and raw techno, its smash-and-grab ambience still represents a perfect snapshot of the time. Liam's musical influences were clear. The breakbeats echoed Public Enemy, only pushed to a seemingly breakneck pace; the sequenced keyboard refrains drew heavily on hip house artists like Renegade Soundwave; while the overall darkness of the sound brought to mind Meat Beat Manifesto's 'Radio Babylon' epic. Together the sounds merged to become a unique version of the hardcore sound of the day. Fast, funky and verging on manic, the title track's lone voice – sampled from a 1940s radio show called *The Shadow* – asking the foreboding question 'What evil lurks in the hearts of men?' had added a feeling of paranoia to it.

There was little doubt that this single was the product of the UK underground rave scene of the time and on its release it sold a healthy seven thousand copies from the racks of the nation's specialist stores. Unlike the plethora of other quality underground releases around this time, 'What Evil Lurks' jumped out at you. In part obviously due to Liam Howlett's musical vision, but also because of the incredible buzz that was starting to surround The Prodigy's performances. Those up-for-it people from Essex; one man and his samplers, one MC and three dancers, dressed to the nines in their dodgy green and white outfits, had started to become a regular and welcome addition to the rave scene. As such, any single they were to release was already guaranteed a high level of enthusiasm from the people who had already seen them.

It was still early on in the band's career and the importance of the live equation was already coming to the fore. Here was a group of people in love with the buzz of doing it, being there. No amount of record sales could beat that great feeling of raving with thousands of like-minded people. And being on a stage, with lasers, lights and smoke machines going off all over the place had quickly turned into the ultimate buzz.

Within days of The Prodigy's debut appearance Ziggy had secured them an impressive list of PAs (personal appearances) and within weeks of the release of 'What Evil Lurks' they were averaging three gigs a week, occasionally even managing two in one night. It was a full-on, hard-working approach to gigging which was to become central to their development. Seeing themselves as a unit on a mission to spread the vibe of The Prodigy, no amount of PAs could dampen their enthusiasm. From that first night The Prodigy were addicted to performing and their hunger for an on-stage fix simply grew.

At the big outdoor events which were at their height during these times, the band would play to audiences of at least five thousand a night. Alternatively they'd play the underground clubs and the illegal warehouse parties which would boast crowds of up to two thousand. These were rave audiences, tuned into the attitude of the band and the atmosphere of the music rather than the spectacle of a band on stage. Completely unlike the kind of crowds who could be found at traditional rock gigs.

The PAs sowed the seeds of the show for which the band are known today. Maxim had quickly become an impressive MC, working with the crowd, building up the vibe with his calls while leaving plenty of space for the music to breathe, his reggae-toasting roots finding a rare harmony with the rave scene. Leeroy, Keith and Sharkey had slowly developed their own spaces as well. Each track would find a different dancer coming to the fore, working off the others but pushing themselves to a new extreme. Leeroy's James Brown stepping was developing nightly, with fresh moves appearing in his repertoire every time the band played. Soon he developed his trademark 'crab-walk' dance which saw him striding sideways across the stage, hips swinging, legs crossing each other and arms waving in perfect time. It was like a streetwise B-boy appropriation of Michael Jackson's infamous moonwalk. Had Pepsi used Leeroy's steps in an advert at the time the youth of Britain would certainly have been found copying the moves in the school playgrounds the next day. It was an invigorating and infectious dance style.

Keith and Sharkey had also added their own unique twists to the dancing-on-the-spot style of the rave. Keith would intersperse his body-twisting moves with bouts of vibing-up the crowd. At this time, vibing-up literally meant smiling, chatting, gurning, anything that would bring about a positive response. Sharkey, on the other hand, had turned her wild-style steps into the perfect accompaniment to Keith.

Although this intense period of gigging would have had most bands bored stupid, looking for an excuse to take a break, for The Prodigy the dates had an added bonus; they were all at places where they would have been going anyway. But there was one rave that the whole posse wanted to do – Raindance. Not just another rave, this was the cream, the Rolls Royce of the rave scene. A chemically charged, lazer-lit and turbo-sound-boosted playground for the E-generation. Indeed Keith has been heavily quoted as saying that, for him at least, Raindance was the highest pinnacle he could have imagined the band reaching. Liam backs this up: 'We did all of the usual places, you know, Astoria, Telepathy and that. We just started to play at our favourite parties; going to these parties and actually playing them. It was amazing. And then we did Raindance and it was like, "OK, that's it. Let's retire now." Being on stage at Raindance, as far as I was concerned, was the absolute bollocks. We played Raindance and, as far as I was concerned, we'd made it then. The set-up was really fucking simple. Literally two keyboards, two big heavy samplers; you'd load the track in and then we'd play it. Three people and a fucking mixing desk. It was just funny. It was humorous. Afterwards, what we used to do, was just go out, and have a good time – dance with our mates. It was a real vibe, man.'

The Prodigy live, although still very basic, was already a fiercely exciting prospect – although it wasn't always perfect. There were nights they played in badly equipped venues with inadequate soundsystems. Or, worse still, the night when almost nobody turned up! It was a mid-week appearance at Hatfield College when The Prodigy discovered the delights of playing to an almost empty room. Although only their fifth gig, they were already used to playing to crowds in their thousands, Liam and crew were little prepared for that fact of real life which besets almost every rock or indie band that ever existed, the 'two men and a dog' syndrome. In this case it was more like five punters and as many bouncers. And little more. Cancelling the gig didn't enter the band's minds; they simply went on and did their thing with as much energy and vigour as any other night. The only difference being the fact that Keith spent the night dancing with the punters.

'We just thought "fuck it, we're here to play so let's rock the place anyway",' remembers Liam. 'Actually it was quite funny really.'

In many ways it was more like a rehearsal for the band. Not that rehearsals were something they ever bothered about. Not since the one time they'd tried to practise round at Liam's dad's house.

'It was a total disaster,' recalls Keith. 'It was like we were some poncy group trying to contrive things, you know what I mean. It just wasn't us – what we needed was that energy and in Liam's gaff, no offence to his Dad, there wasn't no vibe, man. So we just sat down after a little while and had a smoke. No point in carrying on really, so that was the last rehearsal we did.'

It was just prior to this rehearsal that The Prodigy said goodbye to

Sharkey. Increasingly losing interest in the performance, Sharkey's heart lay in actually raving and The Prodigy's demanding schedule started to interfere with her own personal life. It became clear that she wasn't as committed as the others and soon decided to quit the band. Which left The Prodigy as a four-piece – the line up which was to take the name to the international stage.

At this point, however, any plans of conquering the world couldn't have been further from Liam's mind. The Prodigy's one taste of going abroad had been a disaster. It was the summer of 1991 and they were booked to play in Italy. A place they've never since returned to.

'We were completely wrecked in Rome,' confesses Liam. 'It was actually a good gig but the audience were fucking strange. Anyway, the promoter hadn't sorted out our transport so we were just left to sort it out ourselves. We were sitting in the back of this square, with all our equipment and we couldn't get to the airport. And the worst thing was that everyone was completely done in from the night before. I said then I never wanted to go back to Italy. And I've stuck to that.'

The unprofessionalism of one Italian promoter would soon become a distant memory in Liam's mind. The second single had already been recorded, and although they had been playing a version of it since that first gig, in its new, improved form it was set to take the British charts by storm. That track was 'Charly', a single which was to have huge repercussions for The Prodigy.

* * * * *

I go to a lot of raves and I'm forever hearing people moan when a PA is announced. On the other hand, because I'm a raver, I know what they want to see and hear and I'll often come home from a night out and feel inspired to switch on the keyboards and the computer and start to work. The Prodigy is basically all about getting the buzz of a rave onto vinyl.
Liam Howlett in the first-ever magazine interview with The Prodigy
(Melody Maker, 10 August 1991)

Bow, a run-down part of London's East End. A sickly, anaemic glow illuminates the drab concrete of the venue. Under the whisper of pre-club dreariness the club takes on the air of a disused mortuary. The silence is punctuated only by the sounds of people busy organizing.

From the mass of electrical equipment which is the PA comes an occasional crackle, or a loud buzz followed by deafening feedback. 'One two, one two' bellows a technician through a microphone – aping the roadies of the rock world. In one corner the promoter and his friends stand with the excited look of people in control of a small and imperfectly formed church for hedonistic pursuit. It's a typical pre-club affair. The hollow lull before that night's storm.

On the stage Liam Howlett meticulously puts together his equipment. Basic as it is, the task is still done with a surgeon's precision and care. Over by the DJ booth a flu-ridden Keith Flint struggles to keep his mind on the job at hand. He's ill, very ill in fact. The torrential rain outside coupled with the dinginess of the club has filled his heart with a sense of depression. All he wants to do is go home to bed for at least a week. Or maybe longer.

The DJ rifles through his record boxes and pulls out a white label. No writing on it, no clues on the bag either. Keith leans over in interest as the DJ cues up the disc, headphones over one ear. As Keith steps down from the booth and walks towards the toilets the PA suddenly bursts into action. The whole venue is filled with a huge, roughed-up breakbeat animal of a tune. It's electrifying, like nothing that Keith has ever heard before. Hard yet funky, a huge dub-sonic bass line thundering its way through. It seems to Keith that the walls of the venue are rumbling under the strain of the tune.

Momentarily forgetting his illness, an excited Keith runs back up to the DJ booth shouting to the man behind the decks. The DJ is forced to put his headphones down and lean over to Keith so he can hear the diminutive dancer's words.

'What's this fucking tune, man? It's fucking incredible,' exclaims Keith, head already nodding to the beats.

'Fucked if I know, mate,' comes the reply from the somewhat bemused DJ. 'It's your mate up there that's playing it.'

Mouth open wide with amazement, Keith looks up to the stage where, sure enough, Liam is bent over a keyboard, manipulating a sampler. A cold shiver runs down Keith's spine as he realizes that later he will be dancing to the amazing track that is unfolding around him.

This is how it was the first time Keith Flint heard 'Charly'. An unforgettable experience which lifted his spirits and gave him more flu-relief than anything a doctor could prescribe. Only it wasn't the first time. The more Keith listened the more he realized that it was in fact a radically reworked version of a track he'd been dancing to since that first gig. The original version had a massive reggae-style bass line with some ragga-tinged vocal samples. But this new version . . . was something else entirely.

Keith went on to play the gig that night. Pushing his body to an unusual extreme he moved between unbelievable elation and unbearable nausea. By the end of the band's set he vomited, collapsed in a pool of sweat and had to be taken home to Essex in the back of the band's van.

And the venue? A legendary rave club called Telepathy.

'Charly' wasn't a surprise to Nick Halkes and Richard Russell at XL, however. They'd known about this track since their first meeting with Liam. It seemed like a mad idea really. Put a cartoon character on a hardcore tune and sure they'd probably get a novelty hit. But would it also spell the end of the band's career? After all, novelty records are notorious for burying bands for ever.

In the end they had nothing to worry about. 'Charly' was a revelation. A track which worked on so many levels as to provide Liam with a series of escape routes from the novelty cul-de-sac.

The track itself was a hard, underground, house cut. Its breaks were on the cutting edge of breakbeat manipulation. Indeed it was one of the first tracks to cut up the breakbeat in various places in order to create new rhythms. A trick which not only influenced the entire hardcore scene but was also a foundation stone for the jungle sound which was lurking just around the corner.

The vocal sample was of a cat, naturally called 'Charly', taken from a 1970s educational film which placed a young boy with his pet in a variety of situations, in order to warn young children of the dangers in the outside world. Coming as it did at a time when animation had a number of psychedelic overtones the 'Charly' adverts soon took on cult value with the 1970s drug users. Charly was itself another name for cocaine and the adverts seemed to have a sub-narrative which fitted the post-hippy lifestyle of the time.

When Liam happened upon the advert some fifteen years later it was little surprise that he too recognized the psychedelic possibilities. For him, the voices of Charly and the little boy tapped directly into the subconscious air of naive unity that Ecstasy use had placed upon the scene. It was June 1991 and the entire scene was caught up in an almost childlike, chemically induced positivity. 'Charly' seemed to capture this spirit perfectly. Placed next to a hard and dark breakbeat tune however and the potential was for something much more sinister.

'I wrote "Charly" after I'd been larging it up at the Barn Friday night,' explains Liam. 'Saturday morning was always a real fragile time after the drugs from the night before. We used to get up at about ten and they used to show all these 1970s programmes like *The Double Deckers* and things like that. And in between these programmes they'd have these 1970s adverts and that Charly ad would be on every week. I probably was still off my head but I just thought it would be mad to do a track out of that for people who remembered that advert. I also thought it would mess with people's heads a little bit. You know this voice from your childhood giving you good advice in the middle of a fucking rave!

'Cocaine was nothing to do with our scene so I never even thought about those connotations. Everyone was just on an Ecstasy buzz so no-one thought of coke at the time. Although the Es were probably full of coke anyway!'

It was a track which Liam had been wrestling with for months, trying to get right that final ingredient. And, as Keith had already realized that night at Telepathy, the final touches had come with the inclusion of the vocal sample and the changes in bass line. As soon as the record label heard it they were blown away.

'I wrote the tune, and basically played it at Telepathy that night and then went in and played it to XL. They were like, "Yeah, that's the next fucking single." So I went back home and did the rest of the EP.'

The other tracks came together relatively easily. Whereas most artists of the time would have been happy with the main track and placed a substandard cut and a remix on the B-side, Liam was determined that each track on his EP would be as strong as 'Charly'. He was also extremely aware of the fact that 'Charly' itself might not appeal to the underground scene so he decided that the alternative tracks should be full of underground ethos. As a result, 'Pandemonium' was a much harder techno-orientated track, while 'One Love' achieved incredible support from the underground DJs, with its uplifting piano breaks and roughed-up grooves. The final track on the EP was a remix of 'Charly'. Called 'The Alley Cat Mix', it located those childlike voices deep in a dark, tranced-out techno terrain.

Prior to the single's release it had become one of the stand-out tracks in the band's live set, while certain DJs had also caned it. As a result the vibe that surrounded 'Charly''s release was immense. Ravers tuned on to the E-ed-up meeowing cat started to inundate the specialist shops with orders for the single.

'Have you got that one with that kiddies' advert on it?' they asked, as bemused sales assistants checked the release schedules and asked all of their suppliers. But hardly anyone knew what that track was. Even the name The Prodigy turned up blank stares. After all, their single was called 'What Evil Lurks' and that had come out the previous February, some six months earlier.

DJs, greedy to get their hands on a white label of the track, would hassle the record label daily, while some had already put 'Charly' at the top of their DJ charts in the dance magazines, despite never having actually had a copy to play.

Eventually, promo copies started to trickle out and the response was overwhelming. The various tracks on the EP were tearing up raves throughout the country and when The Prodigy played it live, the response went from the usual huge roar of excitement to an almost terrifying euphoria. 'Charly', it would appear, was becoming the chosen anthem for the hardcore ravers. Throughout the country's raves people talked about how massive 'Charly' would be. Indeed, as a direct response to a promo of the single, the *Melody Maker* journalist Push (who would later go on to be the editor of *Muzik* magazine) offered Liam his first chance to be interviewed in a national magazine.

'A lot of my friends have told me that they think the new single will get into the top forty but I hope they're wrong,' Liam confided to Push. 'It's not that I don't ever want to be successful, it's just that I'd rather continue to be an underground act for another two or three records and work on expanding a hardcore following.'

To the surprise of everybody, from Liam through the rest of the band and on to XL, 'Charly' was a huge hit when it was finally released. Sure, they'd expected some kind of chart success, they could feel it throughout the build-up to the record's release. But when it crashed into the national top ten, eventually resting at the number three slot, The Prodigy and their entourage were shocked beyond belief. Liam explains, 'When "Charly" came out I was still working at this printing place, and basically they were joking around saying, "Yeah, you're going to leave us now that you've got records coming out." And then when "Charly"' came out, they couldn't believe it was in the charts. None of them could. I mean, I knew that the track was good and I'd expected it to do well in the dance charts, but this was the fucking national top forty, man. "Charly" was at number three and I was completely . . . gob-smacked. So I went into work and I was like, "See ya later." You know, I didn't care about a steady job. I was having a fucking wicked time every weekend. I wasn't really earning any money and as far as I knew "Charly" could have been a one-off, but I didn't want to be working. I remember my dad saying, "Are you sure? I don't know whether this is cool or not." But eventually he began to really respect the music as soon as he saw it starting to get a bit of recognition.'

With a single in the the top ten, the inevitable chance came to perform on *Top of the Pops*, the UK's longest-running pop music show. Practically an institution, to perform to the hallowed cameras of this BBC show was the dream of almost every aspiring star in the country. But Liam and friends weren't aspiring stars. They came with a set of underground ideals which had little to do with the corporate machinery of *Top of the Pops* and so naturally, in a move which echoed The Clash in 1977, they refused to go on. The producers couldn't understand it, but they *had* to have the fastest-selling single of the week on their show. In the end they opted to show the band's video, a fact which was bizarre in itself since, unlike the majority of the videos shown on the show, week in week out, The Prodigy video had neither a star, nor was it a big-budget production. In fact it was an ultra-grainy, almost home-made show reel of a group of lads . . . dancing! Interspersed throughout was a graphic of the infamous cat adding to the surreal nature of the visuals.

'Charly' went on to sell in excess of 200,000 copies in their home territory alone. The Prodigy had arrived big time.

* * * * *

I first saw The Prodigy at a rave in Stratford, East London, at Telepathy. They were there quite a lot and I saw them many times. For me they were always the highlight of the night because their music was so powerful that you couldn't stand still, even if you wanted to. Watching Keith, Maxim and Leeroy was an amazing experience. The energy they gave off was unbelievable and totally inspiring. It felt like their energy was being transferred into you and that's a feeling I'll never forget.

J. McCulloch, Norfolk, England. Prodigy fan since 1991

September, 1991, Perception (a warehouse somewhere in Cambridge).
It was an empty warehouse. A car auction room according to my mates,
although I wasn't so sure. Anyway the venue had seemed like a million-
mile drive from my home in Nottingham. Over the course of the seven
hours it had taken to find the rave we'd followed bogus direction after
fake location. Got caught up in a convoy of Volkswagens headed,
although we didn't realize it at the time, in the opposite direction and
joined in an impromptu service-station bash just outside the Leicester
turn-off from the M1.

Had this been any other night, we would have stayed, but this night
was to be special. It was a Perception rave. One of the best chemically
addled, house-drenched nights to be had in the country at the time. And
apart from that, those geezers with that song with the cat on it were
playing. And we really wanted to see them. You know, to have a bit of a
laugh at the pop stars. OK, so we'd danced our tits off to the same tune
only a few weeks before, but that was when it was strictly underground,
now it was in the charts it just wasn't worth listening to. That was the
snobbery which surrounded the rave scene, seeping into its smallest
cracks. The Prodigy, we had decided were just sell-out Essex-boys.

Approaching the venue at around midnight, it seemed the entire
countryside was alight. From a distance the air danced with lazers,
picked out by the bellowing clouds of theatrical smoke. None of us were
particularly sure of our exact location (by the time we'd arrived not one
of us was all that together), and to this day I can't be one hundred per
cent accurate. However we suspected that we might be in
Cambridgeshire.

Perception was a like a spiritual experience. Sharing an incredible
buzz with fifty thousand other people was like nothing else on earth. So
many people in one location, unified in a search for that ultimate rush.
High on house music, natural adrenalin and more illegal substances
than the police confiscate in the course of a year's enquiries. Everywhere
I looked a different face grinned back at me, inviting me into the church
of the hardcore raver. Huge eyes projected onto the walls flickered and
rolled with the beats. Colours melted into the air as each nuance of the
music leapt out at me, infinite details becoming one with the whole.
The bass seemed to take on a life of its own, running down my spine and
connecting with my pelvis. I leapt for joy, legs like rubber, heart
pounding like a juggernaut. Deep inside me now the rhythm moved
every inch of my body, synchronizing me with the other forty-nine

thousand, nine hundred and ninety-nine ravers. I was completely lost but still so very much *there*. I was in love with everyone I met, I felt huge surges of lust for the sweating bodies dancing near me, I saw the girl of my dreams – in the distance, just out of reach but still close enough to feel her presence.

Suddenly I became aware of that cat from the advert. The whole place went insane as 'Charly' belted out. 'Hardcore massive – listen up', came the shout from the MC. I lifted my eyes towards the stage and realized that I'd been dancing to The Prodigy. Probably for ages now, I just wasn't all that sure. On stage, a small geezer with long hair was dancing like a maniac, a court jester to the hardcore crew. A basketball-player-tall, black guy danced alongside with legs that seemed even more rubbery than mine and this MC, jumping on the spot, calling out to the crews, pushing the vibe to the edge.

In the middle of all this was a bloke behind some keyboards producing these incredible sounds. As the bass line pummelled my brain and the cartoon cat tickled the hairs on the back of my neck, I decided there and then that 'Charly' was one of the greatest tracks ever. I didn't care who I told it to.

And then it was over. Quick as a flash, but in so much detail that I had to explain everything I'd seen to my mates. I loved The Prodigy that night, no doubt about it. And the next day? I listened to a chart record, a pop hit no less, with a different set of ears.

Perception had happened only a month after the release of 'Charly'. In many ways it was one of the finest statements of intent that the band could have made. No doubt they had rocked the rave that night with fifty thousand of us dancing to their every beat, but they'd also showed how a huge audience made no difference to them. They may have started a few months earlier playing the illegal warehouse circuit, almost tasting the audience's sweat because of the close proximity of the stage, but their destiny lay with huge crowds in massive venues.

With a taste of success on their lips, The Prodigy soon realized that if they were to be considered real players on the scene they'd have to become more professional in their approach. The first change was their manager.

Ziggy had been an excellent help in their formative days, sorting out PAs at some of the finest raves in the land, but at this stage the band needed a strong manager who could take them to the next level.

Someone with experience of big business dealings and a good understanding of the band's underground values. Who better to talk to than Mike Champion, manager of one of the scene's biggest successes of the time, N-Joi?

'I thought I'd better get a manager . . . because Ziggy didn't really do a lot,' laughs Liam. 'So we called Mike Champion, but I just thought "he'll be too busy to be bothered with us". But he agreed to meet us at an N-Joi show. When we got there this bouncer on the door stops us and we all say, "We're with the band", because you know, Mike had said he'd put us on the list. Anyway this bouncer thinks we *are* the band and takes us straight to the dressing room.'

The first person the boys met was the very man they'd come to see. It wasn't long before he'd agreed to take on the band. Something which really shouldn't have come as a surprise to Liam. After all they were in the top ten at the time – any manager who could look this particular gift horse in the mouth and send it packing to the dentist would surely need lengthy sessions on the analyst's couch.

The deal wasn't all that straightforward, however. Mike had a partner. A man with a huge mane of curly hair who, went by the name of Barnet – Mike Barnet. Liam, Keith, Leeroy and Maxim were instantly unsure about him.

'We just used to take the piss out of him all the time . . . couldn't take him seriously. I remember Keith ringing Mike Barnet up and Keith goes, "Hello, is that Mike Bush?" And that's just a typical thing Keith does. He always gets names wrong. He was thinking, it's something to do with hair. Anyway he goes, "No, the name's Mike Barnet", you know, straight as anything. Keith just turns round to me and goes, "We're going to have some fun here."'

What transpired could hardly be described as 'fun'. Although Mike Champion had quickly renegotiated the XL contract in terms more favourable for the band, he was also still embroiled in a lot of dealings with his other act. N-Joi had themselves seen quite a lot of chart action, but things had started to turn a little sour and Champion's skills were constantly in demand from their camp. The Prodigy, Mike reasoned, were in good hands with his partner. Liam has a different story to tell.

'There was a bit of a funny thing going on with N-Joi. I don't know, Mike Champion was away and Mike Barnet, at the same time, tried to be a bit sneaky. He received £15,000 from the record company, my advance for the album. Basically it was paid into his bank account which

I thought would be all right. He gave me £10,000, so an extra five thousand got left in his bank account. I asked for it and when he went to the bank to get it the bank had just taken it because he was in debt to them. So that was that. He ripped me off. He said he was going to pay me back, but he still hasn't done to this day. He was taken out of the management there and then. Then N-Joi split up and Mike Champion was strictly my manager.'

Another change which came about was a far more personal thing for Liam. He moved out of his dad's house.

'My dad was getting pretty fucked off with the amount of noise I was making every night. And then at weekends I'd be out all fucking night. Anyway when I'd been round at this squat that Keith lived in, I'd met a girl, so I ended up going round there a lot. Eventually she moved out and I moved into a place with her. It was partly to get away from my dad. Somewhere I could have a studio and not get moaned at. It's not that he was against my music, he just couldn't stand the noise!'

*　*　*　*　*

'You should have seen them, man, they were like these big kids on their first holiday together,' recalls ex-press officer Leah Riches, clutching the pile of Polaroids of the band from their early days. 'It was the first time they'd been to Germany, so a whole load of us went over, you know, it was more like a family back then, record company, management, crew and band all having a laugh together. So as they were walking down the stairs from the plane to the runway the lads decided to pose like they were, you know, famous celebrities. It was just kids' stuff really, dead naive, but the memory of that kind of stays with me because they were so excited about the whole thing.'

Sure enough, the Polaroid depicts the foursome striking Hollywood poses for the camera. Liam, curly bob and boyish features turned sideways to the photographer; Leeroy, holdall in hand smiling like a millionaire, Maxim staring intensely while Keith laughs like a man who has just found his marbles after years of madness. On the tarmac, a bemused air stewardess looks on, annoyed. Only a harmless prank. Not offensive in any way, but the band were already getting up the noses of the authorities. An occurrence which was to become something of a feature in the life of The Prodigy.

As a snapshot, the Polaroid says little more than 'here's a bunch of ravers off on their holidays'. In reality the band were embarking on their first tour of Germany. It was October 1991 and, amazingly for a band who had yet to release a record outside Britain, the whole tour had already sold out!

Following their earlier experience in Italy the German tour had been approached upon with a certain amount of trepidation by the band. Every step of the way they half expected disasters, so when nothing particularly bad happened they couldn't believe their luck. The only small problem here was the audiences.

More used to the hard nu-beat sounds of Belgium (which were the antithesis of the breakbeat culture of Britain), or the European high-energy sound, the crowds were unsure how to dance. But the band gave it their best shot and they were warmly received.

The first stones of The Prodigy's path to world-wide fame had been laid. What they now needed to do was take on America. But was America ready for them?

* * * * *

I don't want the band to be a one-hit wonder, I'd rather people discovered us gradually and didn't rush out and buy our single.
Liam, Daily Mirror, 27 August 1991

Following the runaway success of 'Charly', the bookmakers' odds were stacked against The Prodigy ever again denting the UK's national charts. After all, over the previous twelve months the dance scene had propelled many a one-off hit from the dingy recesses of the warehouse party directly into the bright lights of the top twenty. Why would The Prodigy be any different in succeeding where countless others had failed? But the cynics hadn't counted on Liam's ability to give his generation exactly what they wanted – hardcore heaven fed directly to the rave main vein. So when 'Everybody in the Place' came out at the end of the year nobody could have predicted that it would go one better than 'Charly' and settle in at the number two slot. It was the busiest time of the year for record sales and subsequently the hardest time to score a top-ten hit, and The Prodigy were at number two! And, more to the point, the only record keeping them off the top slot was a reissue of Queen's 'Bohemian Rhapsody' following the death of lead singer Freddie Mercury. Surely The Prodigy had arrived big time now? All they needed to do was go for broke and stand down on their 'no *Top of the Pops*' rule, and surely the top slot would be theirs, if not for Christmas, then at least in the first chart of the new year. The record company pushed for it. The band still refused. They may have been riding high in the charts, but The Prodigy remained a band of underground principles and doing this kind of television spelled nothing but 'sell-out' to them.

'Everybody in the Place' was a much more commercial affair than 'Charly'. Indeed, in its new, revised form, it showed none of the rawness of the version that had appeared on the 'What Evil Lurks' EP. Much of the darkness had gone and in its place was a funk-fried groove with a high-speed MC calling out the track's title.

Every inch of the track carried the vibe of the current rave scene. The Ecstasy was increasingly being cut with amphetamine or MDA, a much heavier derivative of MDMA (Ecstasy). Indeed the side effects of this latter development left the user 'monged-out' on the floor; eyes rolling and limbs all but useless. These so-called 'smacky' pills were known as Snowballs, and suddenly they seemed to be everywhere, having the complete opposite effect to the desired up-all-night-dancing of real MDMA.

As the drugs changed, so too did the music. The ambience of the tracks became harder and the vocals more intense, sped up to a ridiculous level. Six months later in mid 1992, the harder sound would develop into a style known as 'dark', the proto-jungle style.

Yet 'Everybody in the Place' keyed into the subconscious of those ravers who would boast of taking ten Es in a night. The lads with their shirts off, wearing ski masks to prolong the buzz of the drugs, who had increasingly taken over the raves. The dance music press, eager to jump off the hardcore boat started to call these people 'cheesy quavers' and the rave slowly became devalued.

Much of this devaluation had a lot to do with the inherent élitism in the scene. Raving had become the norm among a large section of the British youth (so much the norm as to put The Prodigy and others in the national top ten) and the original acid house instigators found this hard to deal with.

Like it or not, the full-on and rushing sound of hardcore techno had taken a huge foothold, a position which would have long-lasting and extremely influential effects on the music scene. And The Prodigy were strongly at the forefront of the takeover. For The Prodigy, however, the important thing was to go beyond the safety of the rave scene. In international terms they were merely big fish in a relatively small pond since they were all but unknown beyond the UK. If they were to increase their standing they had to play America.

That was the record label's position. Liam and friends, on the other hand, were just up for the crack of it. So when Mike Champion suggested a trip to New York to play the infamous Limelight club and to film the video for 'Everybody in the Place', they just thought, 'yeah, let's do it!'

'You got to do these things for the experience, haven't you?' says Keith Flint. 'And New York was that all right, you know what I'm saying? It was a fucking experience all right.' That New York experience started in the Big Apple's Limelight club. Notorious for its liberated clientele, the club drew people from all walks of life, just so long as that walk was slightly on the wild side. A hang out for all, from drag queens to leather-clad clones, at this time it was very much the magnet for the city's gay community, along with the wilder celebrities in town.

The Prodigy's music had already made slight inroads into America, thanks to a few imports being picked up by college radio, but, in this Grace Jones-style, disco-friendly club, the band from Essex were most certainly out of place. Musically at least, since it seemed the clothes fit perfectly. Particularly Keith Flint's stage garb of black PVC shorts and more chains than you'd find at your average S&M orgy. Keith felt, to say the very least, worried. Especially when a few of the club clones eyed him up in the toilets.

'Fucking hell man, I just couldn't piss,' he laughs. 'So I had to nip backstage and do it in a bottle. I mean I'm not anti-gay or anything, I'm just not up for it meself.'

Meanwhile, Leeroy was himself hurtling toward an embarrassing moment with a barmaid from Texas who might just as well have been called Tom. Luckily Leeroy realized his mistake before he found out the hard way but it just went to show that maybe there was a side to club life which these Essex ravers had never really witnessed before.

The gig itself went down quite well, with the locals trying their hardest to try and dance to this fast English style, and generally failing miserably. The following day the boys hit the streets to show New York how it was done, for the filming of the video for 'Everybody in the Place'.

It was basically little more than shots of the foursome throwing down a few moves on street corners and messing around in various locations. However, the finished result was remarkable for one thing in particular – it caught Liam Howlett showing off his own fancy footwork. Not to be outdone by The Prodigy dancers he threw a few steps of his own into the hoe-down.

'Liam's actually a really great dancer,' exclaims Leah Riches, eyes wide with excitement at the memory. 'You know, he's kind of cute when he's dancing, A bit self conscious but still really good.'

Leeroy and Keith had little to worry about, though. Liam's shy, stepping antics never made it onto another video!

Back home in England the band continued their relentless gigging. It was a trying time which first showed the boys the downsides of being on the road. For Liam one of these was the simple fact that he didn't seem to have enough time to record any substantial new material. The band were still living off the success of their last two singles, packing out raves everywhere, but Liam knew that the follow-up had to be every bit as good, and original, as its predecessors.

Another downside of the schedule was the ablsolute exhaustion. Something which Liam and Keith remember nearly killing them.

Liam: 'We were in this van driving back from Stoke-on-Trent. We'd played the gig and I remember one of our mates was driving; I'm sitting in the back of this fucking transit van and it was light outside. Leeroy was sitting there, eyes closed, totally mellow.'

Keith: 'Man, the driver was falling asleep at the wheel, wasn't he!'

Liam: 'And I just went, "Fucking wake up, Leeroy, look he's falling asleep." Like it was just humorous. Leeroy suddenly jumped up because he'd been involved in a car accident when he was younger and it had really freaked him out. He was like, "Fucking hell, Uhhh! Pull over!" I hadn't even thought about the danger at that point. I just thought it looked really funny. Anyway Leeroy drove all the way back after that.'

Keith: 'With about a ton of speed to keep him awake! That was pretty funny. The thing is, some of the things that we find funny wouldn't make other people laugh at all. But we thought that was fucking hilarious.'

Over the course of that year, after 'Everybody in the Place' had finally toppled out of the charts in February, The Prodigy saturated the length and breadth of Britain with their sound, while also returning to the States for a brief and relatively well-received mini-tour. Apart from the gigs, however, the only records that came out bearing the band's name were remixes for The Art of Noise and Dream Frequency. The former, a remix of 'Instruments of Darkness' hinted at the possible directions

Liam Howlett could take his music in the future. It was a brooding, dark masterpiece which bore little resemblance to the original. In fact it was so different that many DJs and shops touted the white labels as the new Prodigy single.

By the end of the summer of 1992 things couldn't have been going better for the band, and to top it all off they had signed to an American label, Elektra Records. The joy was short-lived however. In the August issue of *Mixmag*, Britains biggest dance magazine, a feature appeared which could only be described as a hatchet job.

The magazine had a cover photo of Liam holding a gun to his head and a strapline which read 'Did Charly Kill Rave?' The band were naturally incensed. Clearly, when *Mixmag* opted to do this piece there was a separate agenda at work. The Prodigy went in expecting the article to be about their continued success – perhaps even a celebration of the ravers who had made good. However, the feature was ultimately intended as a proclamation of the demise of rave and the subsequent rise of progressive house.

The end of rave had, according to *Mixmag*, been brought about by the proliferation of hardcore tunes with samples from children's TV shows, of which there seemed to be hundreds. Clearly inspired by the runaway success of 'Charly', tracks like 'Trip to Trumpton' by Urban Hype, 'Sesame's Treet' by the Smarties and Shaft's 'Roobarb and Custard' had started to clog up the charts while the raves themselves featured numerous tracks based around the *Magic Roundabout* theme tune, or even the schools' quiz programme of the time, *Blockbusters*, with its competitors requesting letters upon which the questions were based. 'Give us an E, Bob' was as inevitable as it was sad.

When *Mixmag*'s Dom Phillips sought to deride this substandard form of dance music, the target he held up as an example to all was Liam Howlett. The crime: writing the first of the toy-town rave hit 'Charly'. Only The Prodigy track wasn't exactly teeny rave. Even the most untuned ear could hear the production value of Liam's tracks. It was clearly written from an underground perspective and, as has already been pointed out, its influence was far reaching. Unfortunately for Liam and the boys the immediate influence could be heard in these quick-buck, kiddy rave tunes.

But did this make 'Charly' responsible for the death of rave? The immediate question was 'is rave actually dead?' Certainly, thousands of kids throughout Britain would have argued with that statement. Yet it was true that the rave had turned into a pastiche of its former glory, with most of the original party-goers searching for the vibe in new places, like the traveller parties. Others had been lured by the image-conscious club scene of London which still clung to its élitist roots in acid house.

The main motivation behind *Mixmag*'s claim was clearly to separate themselves from rave and align themselves with what they perceived to be the true underground; progressive house. It was just unfortunate for The Prodigy that Shaft or Smarties weren't particularly well known, or they would more than likely have ended up on the cover. The simple fact of the matter was that having Liam Howlett of The Prodigy on the cover would sell issues. Having a strapline which held the band directly responsible for the death of rave would sell even more.

This simple fact of economics was something that Liam could deal with, he even agreed with the sentiments behind the idea that rave had been killed (although, quite justifiably, he couldn't see how he was responsible). What did upset him, though, was the way in which the photograph was secured for the cover, and also the writer's very personal attacks on Keith in the piece.

'To be honest, if we'd carried on making novelty records it would have been all right. You know, if I'd kept on putting out stuff like "Charly", then OK, I'd have put my hands up and said, "Fair cop, you got me." But this was like ages after "Charly", about a year and a half, and I thought those kiddy rave tunes were crap as well. I mean I said once somewhere, "If 'Charly's killed rave then good", and I still stand by that. But Phillips was on a mission; he was out to fuck us up. The whole interview was just tearing into Keith. There was a general bad vibe about the whole thing. I guess it started the ball rolling that the rave scene was going down; that the whole thing was going down. It had got pretty easy to write – take a vocal from here, a sample from there; it wasn't a challenge any more. I didn't really feel like I was writing to my potential so I'd already moved on, but Phillips just wanted to give us a kicking. And the photographer was even worse. He'd got a load of pictures around his studio of these people, all posing with this gun. It was like his thing, you know. So basically he asked if I'd do one for him, for his personal collection. So basically he goes, "hold the gun against your head", and me not being very press-wise, I didn't think about what it would be used for so I just done it. I even said to him, "Send us a copy," because I never thought I'd see it again – it was even done on a poxy little camera.'

Sure enough, despite the full band posing in the studio for a couple of hours in front of the professional standard camera, it was the happy-snappy shot of Liam with the gun that was used, thus providing the band with a very valuable lesson in the ways of the media. And giving *Mixmag* one of their most notorious cover stories ever.

Revenge, as is said, is a sweet thing to taste, and if The Prodigy wanted anything at this time it was revenge. *Mixmag* had stitched them up and they had to show their feelings in some way. With this still in their minds, the band set off to the Welsh countryside to film a video for their next single, 'Fire'.

The track itself lifted the phrase 'I am the god of Hellfire and I give you . . . Fire', from the track of the same name by 1960s artist, The Crazy World of Arthur Brown. It wasn't an unusual sample to lift as, at the same time, Dutch techno artist DHS had a track in collaboration with Jack Dangers of Meat Beat Manifesto (one of Liam's earliest post-hip hop influences), which heavily featured the quote. Liam's version was immediately recognizable as a Prodigy track with its high-speed raw breaks, coupled with a keyboard hook line which was catchier then a rash on a Saturday night and the MC in full flow.

The B-side was even better. 'Jericho' was an adrenalized rush of hyper chipmunk voices wrestling with proto-jungle beats while hook lines sped by and horns floated in the background. With the Genaside 2 remix of 'Jericho', The Prodigy found themselves even deeper in jungle territory – long before jungle had taken off as a popular form.

As a package the new single immediately rubbished any accusations that *Mixmag* may have laid at The Prodigy's feet. Whilst rave may have been a shadow of its former self, The Prodigy were taking the vibe and transforming it.

However, it was with the video that The Prodigy made their most blatant anti-*Mixmag* statement. Filmed under impossible conditions in the Welsh countryside, the film's plot was a simple one; the band sit around a camp fire as the camera isolates them one by one, allowing the direction to go into their own individual psyches. Quite why the film had to be made in Wales was something that nobody appeared to question. And as for the reasoning behind doing it in the dead of night – there didn't seem to be any. The whole experience of making the film was a nightmare, as the band and crew almost suffered from hypothermia; however they did manage to exact their revenge on *Mixmag*. In the closing moments of the film, Liam stands up, leans toward the fire and throws a magazine into the flames. The last frame features the offending issue of *Mixmag* being cremated.

'Fire' came out in September 1992 and was deleted only two weeks later. Yet it still managed to reach number eleven in the national charts. The video however was ditched. The final result turned out to be so bad that the band couldn't bear to be represented by it. It turned out to have been an extremely expensive folly.

*   *   *   *

That first album, *Experience*, it was like our album, you know. It was as if everyone had turned against the rave scene, the police were closing down the parties and the magazines were ignoring it or slagging it, and then comes this amazing album. It belonged to the scene; like it was our trophy that we could hold up to the sad twats who were into that guitar shite and say 'suck on this'. It was really special for the rave scene to have an album that was this good.
Ian Langston, Walthamstow, London. Prodigy fan and raver since
1991

In late November 1992, The Prodigy unleashed their debut album. For a band who lived for the buzz of it all, the title of the album could only be one thing: *Experience*. Packaged in a black and white sleeve, in direct contrast to the multi-coloured images normally associated with the scene, the album instantly stood out as being in some way a quality product.

To The Prodigy's fans most of the album came as no shock, featuring as it did versions of tracks from all of their singles. However the depth of the album didn't lie in the familiarity of the music, as what was more noticeable was the extent to which the tracks had been reworked. 'Charly' had all but the slightest hint of the cartoon cat eliminated, and in its place sat a hard and dark version, exploring the junglist vibe which was growing fast in the underground. It's worth mentioning that 'Charly' was sub-titled 'Trip into Drum and Bass Version'. Whilst some two years later the media would grapple with the notion that drum'n'bass was the new version of jungle, The Prodigy had actually been describing the subterranean sound thus since November 1992.

Elsewhere, 'Everybody in the Place' had taken on a fresher, more vital air about it while 'G-Force' had been all but transformed into a full-on hyper speed anthem going under the name 'Hyperspeed – G-Force Pt 2'. One of the stand-out tracks was the soon-to-be-released single 'Out of Space'. A rough-neck skanking tune with a Max Romeo sample from his track 'Chase the Devil', which displayed Liam's growing fascination with dub and ragga.

The video for 'Out of Space' placed them right at the centre of more controversy. Filmed on a farm, the video featured shots of the boys messing around with Keith dressed as the archetypal raver of the time. Which inevitably meant ski masks with Vicks Vapour Rub taped to it and white-hooded chemical overalls, plus the Keith-inspired addition of pink rubber gloves. With his hood pulled over his head, Keith had an unfortunate similarity to the band Altern 8 who had also adopted this style to promote themselves, while trying to retain some form of anonymity. Keith danced, surprisingly not to the Prodigy track which would feature on the finished version, but to a track by The Sandals – the UK band later to be credited as the godfather of the sound that became known as trip hop, the others were in and out of shot, trying to retake the limelight.

'We weren't really taking the piss out of Altern 8, we were laughing about the rave scene then. It was so far removed from what we were used to, it became a kind of a joke. I was jumping around for a laugh but Altern 8 got paranoid,' explains Keith.

Naturally, Altern 8 saw the video as a dig at them and they proceeded to air their views to anyone who would listen. They even went so far as to mimic The Prodigy in their next video while wearing T-shirts with the words 'Prod Odd Gy' written on them. Liam, Keith, Maxim and Leeroy were all quite flattered by the attention. Altern 8 however were only after some form of revenge.

'Out of Space' was the fourth and in many ways the best Prodigy single to make it into the top twenty so far. But all focus was on the album. *Experience*, whilst not exactly being a classic album, was a strong first step for the band. Coming as it did at a time when dance artists simply didn't release albums, Liam Howlett had nothing from the contemporary scene to use as a standard. As a result he set his own criterion, something which would remain a feature of his work. While offering a perfect snapshot of the time, *Experience* didn't quite achieve the timeless quality that Liam instinctively knew he could achieve. And if there was any proof of the man's true potential, it lay in the album's finest moment, 'Weather Report'.

It is an almost psychedelic episode which begins with a low drone and weather forecasts before opening out into a grandiose, yet sombre strings-led refrain which echoed Tangerine Dream. The track then collapses into a series of abstract noises before launching a down-tempo breakbeat which carries the vibe towards its huge, thundering climax; complete with the full-on, acid madness of a rampant Roland 303 squelching with the intensity of a lightning bolt. A brilliant track which gave a huge hint as to the future direction of The Prodigy. A more complex and assured direction which was moving completely differently to that of the rave scene.

'I remember I had this idea of doing like a rave concept album,' says Liam. 'But in the end I thought it was too restricting. What I wanted was a full experience, you know like you get with one of the early Pink Floyd albums. Something for every mood but still obviously from the rave scene.'

'That first album, it was like, "Fucking hell this is the band I'm in!"' adds Leeroy. 'I was just blown away by it.'

The album entered the charts at number twelve and twenty-five weeks after its release, *Experience* had also blown away the 200,000 people who had bought it. As a result, The Prodigy not only successfully managed to move into the territory of the serious, long-term artists (hitherto dominated by the rock scene) but they also managed to completely sidestep the kiddy rave issue. In so doing they raised a one-finger salute to everyone who had ever doubted them – or more to the point, *Mixmag*. If 'Charly' had really killed rave then The Prodigy were in the process of replacing it with something far better.

*   *   *   *   *

Somewhere in Britain there is a Prodigy fan with unique proof of his devotion. It's probably, quite literally, written all over his face. Or at least permanantly marked like an indentation or a scar. It's a trophy that this Prodigy fan would rather not boast about. It's not an autograph, or a tattoo, it's the band's mixing desk, firmly marked across his visage.

This is how it happened. It was November 1992 and The Prodigy had been on their first full-length tour of the UK since the end of October, promoting *Experience*. Surprisingly, the band avoided the raves and instead opted for using more traditional indie venues. It was a decision that was to display the beginnings of The Prodigy's break from their past with the rave. And one which had been hinted at the previous August when they played the Sound City Festival in Sheffield alongside indie stars Suede and Senseless Things. To the band's surprise the predominantly indie audience took to The Prodigy straight away and the gig was a runaway success. Indeed, the *NME* even went so far as to describe the band as 'A riot . . . The bare stage suddenly becomes a compulsive, multi-faceted entertainment extravaganza. The fascination lies in the layers of sound, the crashing, supremely hedonistic beats which weave to a crazy conclusion. [Liam's] a prodigious master of sound. The future is now.' In other words, the *NME* had, along with the rest of the music press, finally got the picture for what it really was; not a rave thing, not a kiddy hardcore thing, but a Prodigy thing.

The British tour was to a be a twenty-three-date affair with the band taking with them a customized PA and special lasers and lighting. Support came from Sy Kick while three DJs also came along for the experience: Devious D, Physics and Ritchie. It was to be on the last date of the tour that the unfortunate fan gained his unique memento.

The Prodigy show had pulled into Folkestone to play at Leas Cliff Hall. The venue was built into the cliff edge with the roof standing at the same level as the footpath. Consequently all it took for the public to climb onto the roof was a quick shimmy over a small barrier.

The gig had long been sold out, leaving a huge number of Prodigy fans locked outside in the winter cold. Inside the venue the band were going through the pre-gig motions. The sound of the DJs warming up the capacity crowd in the venue became too much for some people, who were clearly angry at not getting tickets. It was at this point that our hapless fan decided to test both his own agility and the strength of the roof. As he edged his way across the roof tiles, a plan hatched in his mind: 'If I get to the skylight I can watch the gig, or even better climb through a window and swing to the balcony below.'

Inside the club the sound of glass crashing to the floor brought a startled silence to the proceedings. As everyone looked up toward the noise, all they could see was a young lad in a Prodigy T-shirt following the shower of glass and tumbling to the floor below. Only he missed the floor completely. Instead he crashed down onto the mixing desk, taking out most of its channels in the process.

A shocked Prodigy crew watched as the fan lay twitching, fearing that he might be close to death. Eventually, the dazed, bloodied and bruised gatecrasher stood up. His trousers were saturated from where he'd pissed himself during the descent. On his face could clearly be seen the indentations of the mixing desk.

'Ten minutes till we're due on and this fan's fallen on our desk!' exclaims Liam backstage. 'Obviously on drugs. Probably thought he could fly.'

'I think the drugs saved him,' adds Keith.

'Imagine explaining that to your mates,' laughs Leeroy, shocked but as usual seeing the funny side. 'He'll be going, "Honest, I got beaten up by some of The Prodigy's gear."'

In the finest tradition of show business the show still went on, despite the mixing desk being reduced to only eight mixing channels. And, in the finest tradition of sod's law, the fan never got to see the gig. Instead he got to look at the four walls of a police cell for the night, having been charged with causing criminal damage.

There wasn't quite the same desperate desire to see The Prodigy on the rest of the tour. On some nights the venues were only half filled, owing to a negligible amount of publicity. The promoters who had come into the business through the raves had very little understanding of the ways and means of promoting a standard gig – even though the band was The Prodigy and the show featured a line-up of DJs. As a result the tour seemed to turn into one of the best-kept secrets of the year.

The Prodigy were therefore faced with financial disaster, their tour barely breaking even. Yet, in the truest sense of the word, the tour was an experience and the band just stood up, brushed themselves down and looked towards the next task at hand: Australia.

*   *   *   *   *

Keith and Liam couldn't resist it. The heat from the Australian sun had become almost unbearable for these two lads fresh from the cold British winter, and the deep blue water looked so inviting. They were standing on a boat, just near the Perth Bridge when finally the call of the cool sea got the better of them. They jumped in, head first. The water was freezing.

'See you at the bridge, mate,' laughed Keith as he settled into a mean crawl. Liam took the challenge and quickly followed. The race was on. The prize? Honour, pride . . . and the chance to boast about the conquest for the rest of the tour.

As Liam looked back he could clearly see the hull of the huge boat.

He soon realized that the water was a lot deeper than he had at first thought. Turning his mind back to the race he looked across toward the bridge. The boat had been moored about 1,500 yards out and he still had at least a third of that to go. Suddenly he noticed Keith in the distance spluttering. 'I'm not going to make it,' he shouted as tiredness took over his body. But all Liam could think was 'shit, we've got to make it or we won't be able to do the gig tonight'.

Eventually Keith returned to the boat and dragged his exhausted body out of the water and back on deck. An equally tired Liam soon followed. As the pair of them sat there they contemplated how close they had come to the real death of a Prodigy dancer.

'Yeah, but what a buzz!' exclaimed Keith. The two of them burst out laughing. It had been a buzz all right.

On 26 December 1992, The Prodigy arrived in Melbourne to play their first gigs down under. Originally they had been booked to play on the same bill as Carl Cox. Unfortunately they had to pull out of that bill and were given instead the dates with Sasha and Paul Oakenfold.

Putting The Prodigy on the same bill as Sasha is strange enough, but to have Oakenfold as well was sheer madness. Sasha and Okenfold specialized in US house music and all of the élitist snobbery that went with it. In clubbing terms they were the complete antithesis to Liam's beat barrages. The mood on the tour was, to say the least, tense.

'Every day we wouldn't get on the same bus with him and he would blank us,' explains Liam. 'Two years later, once we'd got a bit of respect he was like, "Hey, wanna come to Australia" you know, having a laugh. But back then we weren't cool enough for him. I like 'im, he's all right now. I just laugh at it.'

Things reached a head on New Year's Eve when Oakenfold played the infamous 'Sesame's Treet' immediately before The Prodigy took to the stage. It was an obvious reference to the *Mixmag* débâcle, and it had the band up in arms. But it was only a short five-day tour and within a week the boys would be back in America, so they decided to grin and bear it – in the meantime throwing in an endless stream of jokey banter aimed primarily at Oakenfold, the DJ they had dubbed 'Floor Clearer'.

If they thought sharing a tour bus with Paul Oakenfold was difficult then what lay in store for them on the US tour was decidedly beyond the pale. This time their companion was Moby, the vegan, Christian, antismoking techno star from New York. Not a particularly comfortable pairing, considering the Essex lads' reputation for living it up and smoking more ganja in a day than the British customs seize in a year. Friction was almost inevitable, especially since the tour was to last twenty-eight days, providing The Prodigy with only two days off on their thirty-day visit. And even then those two days were to be taken up filming a video for 'Wind it Up', the next single to be lifted from *Experience*.

The tour had been arranged by Moby's manager of the time and although it could be said that she had shown an immense amount of vision trying to convert America to the delights of techno music, it could also be said that her organizational skills left a lot to be desired.

'That was the first proper US tour we did and we got really ripped off badly,' sighs Liam. 'All we cared about was the music. Going to America wasn't really real. We weren't that bothered really so when the idea of the tour was suggested we just went along with it for the crack. But the girl that was organizing it – Moby's manager – she wasn't interested in what we were doing . . . and we were headlining!'

Perhaps the first realization that all was not as it seemed was when the band saw the tour bus. Belonging to the 1970s Adult Oriented Rock band The Eagles, it had the legend 'Hotel California' airbrushed along its side panels. Not a great start for a rolling techno revue – a coach named after one of the most tedious rock songs of all time!

Even worse was the continued conflict between the straight-edged Moby and his travelling companions.

The Prodigy don't deny that they have always been partial to a little smoke, and this tour was no exception. Unfortunately Moby didn't partake of the dreaded weed. In fact he hated all kinds of smoke with a passion. It was an instant case of chalk and cheese.

'There was the big lounge in the coach. He kept moaning that he was getting stoned lying in his bunk-bed because of the air conditioning. He kept on banging on the door and going, "Hey guys, c'mon." He was just like really pathetic. Nice guy and all that, but I couldn't get on his wavelength, although I have to say I did actually like him. He was just a really straight American. All his records were like Kraftwerk and early Human League, you know what I mean? He was straight techno. But our thing wasn't just techno, it was party music. And he wasn't what you'd call a party animal!'

If coping with Moby's idiosyncrasies had been the only thing that the band had to deal with on the tour then it would have been fine. Unfortunately, from the moment the band landed on US soil, things started to go wrong.

They had been booked to play a gangsters' bar in LA who threatened them not to play at a rival promoters venue the following night. On the way to Dallas the tour bus broke down and they were forced to hire a plane – or to be more accurate, a bathtub with wings. They'd been ripped off at every venue and to add to their misery they were absolutely knackered. There had to be better ways of conquering America but at the time the band couldn't see beyond whether or not they'd get paid that night.

Leeroy was particularly angry about the whole deal. As the tour went on, the usually high-spirited dancer sank deeper and deeper into an angry depression.

'It was pure hell,' recalls Leeroy. 'We were working our arses off for nothing. And to make matters worse we were all getting ill. I nearly packed it in so many times on that tour. I mean, if it hadn't have been for the fact that the band were my mates, and Liam's music was so fucking good I would have just done a runner – come back home and tried to forget about it all.'

'We just thought "I never want to go there again",' adds Liam. 'It was just a shit time for all of us.'

By the time the tour reached Toronto in Canada, things were at breaking point. Maxim was so ill that he was forced to miss the gig and the rest of the band were so fed up that it was almost impossible to give their usual one hundred per cent. They'd played over seventy gigs since November 1992 and the strain of it all was beginning to show.

At the end of February 1993, The Prodigy returned home, a far more dejected band than the one who had left the country. However soon after they arrived back the foursome were awarded gold discs for *Experience*. In light of recent events the award seemed to have more than a hint of irony about it.

*   *   *   *   *

It was now March 1993 and the record label had already decided to put out another single from the album, to act as a stop gap until Liam could record some more material. That single was 'Wind it Up', a choice Liam wasn't too happy with. For a start, it meant that another track from the album was out as a single, which was the kind of thing of thing the mega stars like Michael Jackson were doing. It was, to Liam's mind, a rip-off for the fans. His other reason for being unhappy lay in the musical nature of 'Wind it Up'. It was another breakbeat track, released at a time when The Prodigy as a whole had lost interest in raves and Liam had begun to want to take the music in other directions.

The single also had bad memories attached to it because the video had been filmed during that ill-fated US tour. Another film based around the boys messing around in various locations around LA and Venice Beach, the 'Wind it Up' video also featured footage of Keith nearly having a premature meeting with his maker at the hands of the sea.

Standing on top of a wave breaker on Venice Beach, Keith hit upon the idea of being engulfed by the water. In his mind, the waves would probably only reach his ankles so it wouldn't be that dangerous. The first couple of waves came and went no problem. Keith was standing with his back to the sea awaiting instructions from the smiling crew and band. Suddenly the entourage just stared in horror. What Keith didn't see was the huge wave, three times his height, looming large behind him.

'I don't think he'd realized how big the waves were,' laughs Liam, 'I mean, there had been a warning on the radio, but we just kind of ignored it and . . . '

'And everyone was going, "Wave, wave,"' interrupts Keith. 'Suddenly, all I could see was their mouths open with no words coming out. I didn't hear anything. And then there was water crashing all around me. It crashed down and swept in, taking me with it. That was quite mad. Actually I was shitting myself.'

But the director was happy, so Keith's condition didn't matter!

THREE
The Rhythmical Remedy

It was the summer of 1993. The rave scene was dying on its feet and Liam Howlett, long since disenchanted with the whole thing, had his sights set on musical expansion. The release of a fifth breakbeat-orientated single from the album hadn't helped one bit. No matter how good, 'Wind it Up' was at least a year old when it made it onto twelve-inch and by that time the breakbeat sound of hardcore was beginning to sound extremely dated. The scene had moved forward, with many exploring the darker elements of jungle techno, whilst others moved further into house territory.

For Liam, the next stage of The Prodigy's development meant incorporating a far wider musical palette. The main problem was how to push forward without the eyes of the underground and the media analysing their every move. Thanks to their overwhelming and sustained success, The Prodigy elicited an incredible amount of snobbery from people. As such, anything they were likely to do next would be sure to be slagged off in print and ignored in the clubs. The way out of this conundrum was in fact quite an obvious one. Liam had to go back to the DIY roots of the underground, in order to play them at their own game.

Since returning from the American tour Liam had been working constantly in his home studio. Ideas were being thrown around at random, different flavours added to take things in a different direction. At first it was hard, breaking down some of the tricks which had become central to his way of working. The breakbeat had to become less important, even though it had been the backbone of everything he had released so far.

First of all, however, Liam had a remix to do for a new act called Emanation, for which he was being paid in equipment. As he badly needed some new gear to continue to progress, he agreed, even though he wasn't particularly keen on the original version. One morning, as he was creating some new sounds to work on the remix, the new Prodigy sound he had in mind came together.

'I started working on it and thought "that's good, I'm keeping that", and put it to one side for myself. In the end, I spent like a day doing another mix for them. Actually it was still pretty good so I nearly kept that one for myself as well.'

The tune that Liam had put to one side for himself was a hard, house-based affair with Arabic-sounding refrains and heavy percussion. For the first time in months Liam had produced a track which he felt represented a radical step forward. But would the press give it a chance? And would the DJs play it out?

Soon after completing a second, mellower version of the track, Liam pressed it up onto a plain white label with an address hastily scribbled on it. The promo label also contained the name 'Earthbound 1&2' on it in order to further hide the originations of the track. As soon as the whites were distributed through the subterranean grapevine of the underground scene the track created an incredible buzz. DJs played it constantly while the dance press went out of their way to praise it. 'Earthbound' became one of the soundtracks to that summer. Liam Howlett had pressed all the right buttons to cause the underground to react. Everyone wanted to know the truth about the origins of 'Earthbound'. He'd played them like puppets.

When promos for the next Prodigy single started to appear towards the end of the the summer, the truth finally came out. Earthbound was the name of Liam's studio. The track, actually called 'One Love' had its official release in October of that year. As soon as the cool crews, the self-appointed taste-makers of the scene who had ranted about the genius of 'Earthbound', realized that it was The Prodigy behind the record, they dropped it like a shot. They didn't want to be associated with a chart band. The Prodigy just laughed; the record had proved a point; that they could still kick on the underground.

But how would the fans react to this new direction? In order to remain true to Liam's original ethos of putting different styles of track on every single release, the official version contained the much heavier 'Rhythm of Life' along with 'Full Throttle' and a Johnny L mix of the title track, both of which were far more in line with the older, hard breakbeat style of the band, which should have appealed to the fans,

Liam needn't have worried as 'One Love' reached the number eight position in the national charts. Still in retrospect Liam suggests that it wasn't much more than a filler single while he was getting his head together to record the next album.

'It was an in-between song. The B-side was more relevant, which was like a punk track. God knows why we released "One Love" but at that time we didn't know what we could get away with. Not that we were trying to cater for the clubs but it was at a time I thought that nobody was interested in us on the underground any more. We put this white label out called "Earthbound". The thing is, at the time no-one in the band particularly liked the song apart from me. The reason Leeroy and Keith hated it was because it wasn't dancy enough. I still don't know why I put that one out. I should have listened to Keith and Leeroy because I think "Full Throttle" was far more where we were headed.'

If putting out the single had seemed like a mistake, then the video was nothing short of a disaster. In a massive attempt to break with the past, The Prodigy moved away from the usual shots of the boys dancing in various locations, opting instead for state-of-the-art computer graphics.

The finished promo depicted an Aztec city with only computer-generated images of the band. Indeed, the images of Leeroy and Keith had converted their art to a few staggered and jerky movements, reducing their steps to the level of a two-dimensional cartoon movie. They weren't into it at all. Neither was Liam.

'It just didn't fit with the music at all. And I think it looked really tacky, kind of like an advert or something. But a lot of TV shows played it so it must have had its qualities,' reasons Liam.

In fact, the 'One Love' video became a regular on MTV. Even though the underground dance show, *Partyzone*, had long supported the band this was the first time that one of their singles had made that crossover into the mainstream shows.

'We were doing stuff on The Prodigy long before anyone else was interested in them,' recalls *Partyzone* producer James Hyman. 'We'd given every single as much space as possible and we did these specials on them. Nobody else on television was prepared to stick their necks out for the band, but I knew they were special from the first time I heard "What Evil Lurks".'

With 'One Love' achieving MTV support the band found themselves gaining a strong European following. Indeed the video successfully consolidated the results of constant PAs in Europe throughout the summer. After the rave the kids may not have known who those people were they'd seen up on the stage, but as soon as the track was played on MTV, the jigsaw quickly came together.

The Prodigy played almost sixty gigs over the course of that summer. It was a heavy schedule which took them the length and breadth of Britain and to much of Europe. Two gigs stand out as being particularly memorable. The first came when they were booked to play in Greece. It was to be one of the scariest gigs the bands have ever played to date.

Liam recalls, 'We were supposed to be playing in this quarry. It was a really big venue with a capacity of about 6,000 people. We got to about the last but one song and basically looked across; there were about thirty guys in crash helmets. Just guys, not police, but normal people throwing rocks into the crowd and on the stage. I remember Leeroy got on stage and started a fight with one of these dudes but it wasn't worth it, because there were so many of them. It was just like, "Shit, let's get the fuck out of here!" Loads of people were getting hurt, but most of the crowd were oblivious to what was going on. They couldn't see what was happening. We left the stage and got into this room and all these pigs started coming in. And people didn't know why we'd left and they crowded the stage and came and started throwing things around back stage. That was pretty scary.'

At the time the band thought that they might have been the problem. Perhaps the lads in the crash helmets didn't like dance music. Or perhaps they were from a right-wing group which took offence at the colour of Leeroy and Maxim's skins. In the end they discovered that the altercation could be put down to a local promoter who had also wanted to put on The Prodigy. Nevertheless the band refused to ever play there again.

'I don't really like playing hot countries anyway,' claims Liam. 'So missing Greece out is no great loss.'

The second date which stood out from that summer was perhaps to be one of the single most important turning points in the band's career. It was in Scotland at a rave called Resurrection – or 'The Rez' as it's also known. (Ironically it was promoted by John Fairs who was to become the band's tour manager soon after.) Based in Edinburgh, this rave was one of the many legal events which had sprung up over the last couple of years and, as such, was subject to stringent laws governing sound. When The Prodigy went on stage to do their show the representative of the local council kept forcing the sound to be turned down. Eventually the band were so quiet that conversation was easy and planes could be heard flying overhead. It was one of the worst possible conditions for the band to play in.

'It was really fucking awful,' recalls Leeroy. 'Planes, cars, even the audience were louder then us.'

In the end, The Prodigy were forced to take the unprecedented step of abandoning the gig. But the noise restrictions weren't the only thing that got to Liam.

'I remember just looking out across this crowd and seeing all of these kids wearing white gloves with light sticks and that. All these fucking idiots and I just thought "this has nothing to do with us any more". We'd moved on.'

But the band still believed vehemently in the right to party. It was their roots, their reason for being. Consequently they felt increasingly disgusted by the pressure the authorities were placing on the rave scene. Rather than just sit around complaining about the sorry state of affairs and not actually doing anything, Liam decided that 'One Love' had to carry the 'Right to Party' message. He subsequently printed a 'Special Announcement' on the back of the sleeve for 'One Love'. In effect it was an attack on the authorities and an apology to the fans who had paid good money to see them play, and had then been unable to hear them properly. The special announcement read:

'Remember a few years ago? Remember the raves with the pumping bass, the volume at its best, the atmosphere kicking, the people friendly and free! But the police had to put their oar in. The government had to have their say, "Turn down the music noise pollution." What a load of bollocks.

'If you've been to the latest raves then you'll know the score. What's going on? You pay between 15-25 quid. Queue up for about 45 minutes whilst having to put up with the old bill eyeing you up and down as if you're some sort of mass murderer. And once you've been searched and had your shoes and socks removed, you then walk into the grounds to be met by thousands of police and the music at about 2 DBs. You might as well have brought your Walkman.

'At every large rave lately the department of health and environment are there with their precious little toys called BB meters, making sure the volume doesn't go above a certain level. For example if you went to Universe on 13/8/93, Resurrection on 14/8/93 or Living Dream on 6/8/93 then you'll know what we mean. All we can do is apologize to you all for the very bad sound quality. But what can we do? You can't blame the promoters because they are doing an excellent job of bringing you the best quality sound system (even though you don't get to hear it at its best). Authorities have two methods of getting them to turn it down – 1. They can revoke the licence and close down the party and then ban any further events by the offending organization. 2. Impose ridiculous fines which could be in excess of £25,000 and revoke any future licences.

'Now you know why these events are becoming more and more of an effort to go to. And why they're so quiet when you do.

'So there's no-one left to blame but the authorities. Bollocks to the authorities. You can't stop us. We're gonna keep the dance scene strong even if the world isn't. This is your day and no-one can take it away from you. The dance scene is far too big to just disappear.

'Respect – Liam, Leeroy, Maxim, Keith, Mike (Prodigy/ Midi)'.

It was a strong message and one which needed to be said, but it also inadvertently placed The Prodigy in the middle of the political arena. As the changes in the laws came in to play, so a whole generation of ravers were being turned into criminals for the way they chose to spend their leisure time. People from the scene were feeling increasingly disenfranchized by society and they desperately needed figureheads to look to. Enter The Prodigy.

*   *   *   *   *

It was the beginning of 1994, The Prodigy had scored six top-twenty hits in the UK, they'd been awarded a gold disc for their debut album *Experience*, had toured much of the world, and still their average age was only twenty-three. With the amount of success The Prodigy had already seen it now fell upon Liam to take things forward. For the first time since the band had formed they took a lengthy rest from performing so that Liam could get to work on the next album.

Liam's methods of recording the band's music had changed little since those earliest days. Initially, he had started recording on a basic piece of equipment called a Roland W30 workstation keyboard and a small eight-track mixer. Utilizing the decks he already owned, he simply sampled stuff by using the decks as a source, then mixed the samples in with the original music he was recording. It was using this method that had secured him the deal with XL on the strength of the

'What Evil Lurks' demo tape.

Liam next added a Roland U220 RS PCM sound module to his set-up, a sound bank which stored different sounds on it. Incredibly it was from this piece of equipment that Liam found the piano for 'One Love'. Furthermore, he created 'G Force' while he was messing around with it one day. For added effects he included an effects unit called a Quadraverb which enabled him to broaden his style somewhat. The next keyboards he added were a Roland Juno 106 and a Juno 2, and he also brought on board a TB 303 to create the bass line. The 303 was the piece of equipment essential in the creation of acid house and as such its sound was almost universally known. For Liam, the challenge was to use it for its strengths rather than simply let it take over, like so many other producers at the time had done . For drum sequences Liam also included a Roland TR 909.

At a time when the dance scene seemed completely in awe of the ubiquitous Atari and sequencing software, it came as a surprise that Liam didn't actually use the set up.

'One of the reasons I don't use an Atari is that if something is hand made, it comes out better,' he explained to *Music and Technology* magazine at the time. 'With the W30 I can tap in exactly what I want – I never use copy mode, never. I think with an Atari it's just too easy to tap in a bass line, repeat it for thirty bars and so on. Instead of having the same cymbals all the way through I rap them in and change them as I go. And I think that helps give me "my" sound. I talked to another local group, Shades of Rhythm, about it and they couldn't believe it. I was going to buy an Atari but there's no point.

'I like to tap in sequences really, really simple. Like I may take a really simple bass line and build the track around that. The ideas can come from anywhere – I was listening to a Deep Purple record the other day and there was a bit of drumming in there that I really liked so I took it and built the whole track around that because there was so much excitement in it. It's hard to say that I've got a formula because I may start with a piano riff and build it up around that. But if you listened to a couple of tracks I think you could tell they were by me because they would have a similar construction.'

After 'One Love', Liam knew that he would have to take things away from the band's earlier sound, although he wasn't sure where that new direction lay. One thing he was certain of was that he was going to be introducing a much wider style base. And this didn't just mean incorporating aspects of house, trance or ambient into the soup. No, what Liam was aiming for was a much more eclectic mix which would include the new influences he'd started to take on board. Like rock music.

'When we were doing all of these shows in America I started listening to a lot more guitar-based stuff,' he explains. 'Up until then I'd always ignored anything that was in any way rock because it just meant leather jackets and greasy hair to me. Then I heard *Nevermind* by Nirvana and it just blew me away.'

It's little surprise that Liam was so taken by the album that created an international grunge explosion. Not only did the album contain a very similar energy and power to The Prodigy, but it also used layered sounds in order to create more tension; one of Liam's trademarks as well. The instruments may have differed but the sentiment was certainly the same. Nirvana weren't the only rock band that Liam discovered during this time. He also got into artists as diverse as The Beastie Boys, Rage Against the Machine and, more surprisingly, Queen. Or, to be accurate, Queen's soundtrack to *Flash Gordon*.

'OK, so the main track's bollocks,' he argues, 'but you just have to listen to the rest of the album to understand why I loved it so much. There's just loads of really cool detail and these brilliant textures. It was a really inspiring record purely for the orchestration of it. But at the time I was listening to so much stuff, you know, rock stuff like Ted Nugent and old funk stuff as well like the JBs so it was inevitable that my sound was going to kind of reflect this.'

With Liam bursting with new ideas, work on The Prodigy's second album started quickly. He had soon put down two slow-burning songs, tracks which were more experimental than anything he'd ever tried before. And then . . . nothing. Liam dried up totally. His answer to this previously unknown writer's block was to go snowboarding.

The adrenalin-inducing sport was exactly what he needed. One of the problems Liam had come up against was the simple fact that he vibed off the love performance. The energy of it was in itself a huge influence. Back in Braintree the studio didn't give him the right buzz.

In an attempt to capture an essence of those early warehouse gigs, while also tapping into the rock'n'roll heritage that was increasingly a part of Liam's life the band also took this time to play a one-off gig – in London's infamous Marquee Club. It was to be an incredible night with the band and fans turning through a thousand variations of euphoria.

The Prodigy cauldron was cooking again.

Liam returned to work on the album a month later, with a deadline of July 1994. He'd called in an outside engineer to work on some of the tracks. Neil McLellan had impressed Liam with his work on N-Joi's 'Adrenalin' EP and Liam initially called up McLellan to help on 'One Love'. The pairing was a fruitful one with the two musicians working very well together. So much so that McLellan ended up working on five of the tracks from the album.

In May 1994 the first new single from the long-awaited second album arrived in the shape of '(No Good) Start the Dance'. It wasn't exactly brand new to the fans as numerous early versions of the track had been a feature of the band's PAs for quite a while now. The main difference, however, lay in the vocal line.

For months, Liam had wrestled with every aspect of the track. He knew that it had potential but somehow he just couldn't find the right key to unlock the door to it. He'd tried slowing the beats down, tried a variety of different beats. What he hadn't tried was a vocal line.

In the end he placed a female vocal over the track. It provided the hook he'd been looking for, but it also brought with it a few doubts. The female vocal hook-line had become almost standard fare in the dance scene, with artists like 2 Unlimited achieving international success with the formula. Liam feared that using a similar device would take him in almost the opposite direction that he wanted to be travelling in. He vowed it would be last female vocal track he would do.

'(No Good) Start the Dance' was easily The Prodigy's most poppy release to date, achieving the number four slot in the charts. But it also proved to be incredibly popular with the fans. Indeed, it became the band's last song at every gig they did for the next couple of years. The encore tune which came with an open invitation for the audience to climb on stage and party.

If '(No Good) Start the Dance' failed to take the band in a startling new direction, the the video certainly did. Set in an underground warehouse, the black and white promo features the band wandering through disparate groups of people taking in the scenes. Eventually the band go into their own spaces and start to do their own thing. It's a snapshot of the band's personalities; an abstract biography which is to set the tone for the future performance of the band. Keith starts the video with that usual laid-back and friendly vibe until suddenly he turns into a madman straining at the leash. Liam walks to a wall, picks up a sledgehammer and starts pummelling away at the brickwork and Leeroy takes over the dance floor with a display of manic dancing. Meanwhile Maxim observes the whole thing, watching through cat's-eye contact lenses. The video climaxes with Keith being locked in a smoke-filled glass box.

It proved to be a brilliant promo which not only marked out the band from all of their peers by highlighting individuals over the collective, but it also hinted at the incredible theatricality of The Prodigy, something which had only recently started to come to the surface during the PAs, but which would become powerfully evident on the forthcoming album *Music for the Jilted Generation*.

*   *   *   *   *

A huge canyon cuts a wound in the countryside, creating a divide which is impossible to traverse without a bridge. On one side of the divide a city belches poisonous fumes as a dull orange sky silhouettes a mess of industrial buildings, chimneys and tower blocks. At the edge of the city side of the canyon stand hundreds of riot police, hiding behind shields, shouting commands and waving batons.

The object of their anger stands on the other side of the divide. A long-haired traveller, complete with cut-off denims and paramilitary boots raises a middle finger to the authorities as, in a last act of defiance he takes a machete and slices through the ropes on the only bridge across the canyon, thus cutting off any potential access for the police. In the background a huge soundsystem stands in the middle of a green meadow, as thousands of people dance. The traveller has saved the free party from the bigoted intolerance of the authorities.

The messages in the painting are clear. The utopian ideals of the rave are about purity and joy of life while the dystopian city image evokes a sense of power, greed, corruption and pollution. The green meadows of the rave offer the best route forward for those able to tune into its vibes, although the right to party has to be fought for. However, when this powerful image is placed inside the sleeve of the second album from the biggest act to have emerged from rave at the same time as the government are introducing the Criminal Justice Bill which will outlaw all ravers, travellers and free party people, then the semiotic message becomes increasingly political.

Add to this the title *Music for the Jilted Generation* and the message couldn't be any clearer. Not for the first time, The Prodigy had been drawn into the political arena, and this time they would seem to have made the most direct statement against the Criminal Justice Act ever. Except that the album had little to do with this government legislation. It was an album which was meant to have far wider implications. The ravers were the jilted generation, outlawed by police, the media and in many cases by youth themselves. This album was intended to be about the coming of age of Liam and his contemporaries, but the campaigners against the government saw it as a rally to arms and a standard for them to bear.

'It didn't ever occur to me that it was a Criminal Justice album,' recalls Liam. 'I'd hate to be accused of jumping onto a political bandwagon for my own gain. We'd already experienced so many things on the party scene, repressing what we were doing. Like going on stage in Scotland and the officials turning the sound right down and that but I wasn't actually against the Criminal Justice Act. Not all of it. When you look at it there were some good things that they wanted to introduce but what they did was bring in the anti-rave bit on the back of other things. What I was against was any legislation which outlawed the free party scene.'

With the common perception of The Prodigy suddenly becoming politicized, it wasn't long before other activists wanted to adopt the band for their own cause. In one well-reported case the following year, activists campaigning against the M11 motorway extension wanted to use a Prodigy track on a compilation album. Liam wasn't having any of it, even going so far as to say that he had no feelings for these hippies who live up in trees.

'All of sudden people wanted to use the tracks for the M11 protest and stuff and we didn't give a fuck about that. Why should I give a fuck about that, it's not my concern. Well, more to the point, I don't want to become a spokesperson for it. What the protester did was confuse the anti-M11 campaign with the anti-CJB campaign. And then they've mistaken us for a political band. The album wasn't written for the Criminal Justice Bill, it was about anger and I didn't want the tunes passed around to these people living up trees and stuff. They were saying the vibe about the band is so big among the campaigners. To be honest I felt a bit bad when I said I don't care about the people living up in the trees. I shouldn't have said that maybe, but it's got nothing to do with what we're about. I'm not a traveller. I don't need to worry about protecting the travellers. People thought we were spokespeople for the whole thing and we weren't.'

Music for the Jilted Generation was light years ahead of the debut album. Far more assured, experimental and eclectic. The album's intro featured the sound of someone hammering away at a typewriter before a voice announces, 'So I've decided to take my music back underground, to stop it falling into the wrong hands.' It was a statement of intent for Liam. No longer was he a part of any particular scene, The Prodigy had transcended any limitations imposed by particular genres, and instead he took whatever he wanted, from whichever genre he wanted to create music that was The Prodigy and not a representation of a particular scene. In a sense therefore, the painting contained in the album sleeve could also have been seen as Liam burning his bridges and moving onto pastures new.

'I remember thinking I wanted to do some kind of concept album, and at least an album that had almost like a picture on it; a group of songs which fitted together somehow,' recalls Liam.

With a relative lack of breakbeats on the album the range of styles, tempos and flavours was incredible. From the darkly brooding delinquency of 'Break and Enter' to the hard and fast techno metal of 'Their Law' (which featured post-grebo sample hooligans Pop Will Eat Itself), from the up-tempo, techno soundtrack rush of 'Speedway' to the down-tempo B-boy grooves of 'Poison', the album displayed Liam's genius in a way that all those around him had always claimed he was more than capable of.

One of the most outstanding aspects of *Music for the Jilted Generation* was the freedom Liam had discovered. Freedom in sound which enabled him to explore ideas, unhindered. Nowhere is this more clear than on the concept section of the album. Collectively called the 'Narcotic Suite' it was made up of three separate tracks which moved from the 1960s film noir soundtrack of '3 Kilos', through the techno hedonism of 'Skylined' and then into the deep, suffocating grooves of 'Claustrophobic Sting'. It's a sequence of tracks which saw Liam moving through styles with the agility of an athlete.

Yet, despite its variety, the album is incredibly cohesive. This is perhaps the first time when Liam's ability to see the greater picture of the album came into play. To him the album was to tell a complete story and each track was like a piece in a jigsaw puzzle. In this way he could get away with changing styles from one track to another, just so long as it flowed as a part of the whole.

Liam was in for a shock when he went to master the album, however. Convinced that the album was going to be a success in its finished state, when he got to the cutting room he discovered that he'd actually recorded too much material to fit on one CD. All of that time spent compiling the album to create a thread throughout and now he had to cut tracks. Ultimately, the live favourite 'We Eat Rhythm' had to be cut entirely. 'The Heat (The Energy)' had to be edited right back, as did 'One Love'. Surprisingly however, despite these changes to the original planned album, Liam actually thought that this edited version worked better. It was somehow more direct and the theme flowed a lot easier.

The album's release in July 1994 was met by a hugely positive response from fans and critics alike. It represented a step forward for Liam who could no longer be accused of being nothing more than a rave producer. Although this has always been a completely inaccurate criticism of him, with *Music for the Jilted Generation* Liam displayed a musical ability which betrayed a very real talent for the epic.

For the people who had followed the band this album mirrored a growth that they had all gone through. The Summers of Love had turned out to be little more than a hollow ideal, and besides, everyone had grown up since the early days. The Prodigy had matured right alongside their contemporaries.

'One of things I loved about it was the fact that the tempos vary loads,' explains Leeroy. 'I mean, you've got your fast stuff but then there's the things like "Poison" which is only about 105 bpm. At one point I was just getting tired of all the beats getting fast. I remember saying to Liam at the time, "You don't have to do stuff fast for it to be hard." I mean it was getting hard to keep up with them. When we started playing the slower stuff live it meant we could get into some more steps and vibe with it more.'

The critics were turning cartwheels to find new superlatives to describe this ultimately modern album. UK magazine *Select* called it 'the best electronic pop record you'll hear this year', and for months the press would hold it up as the very paradigm of technology-based music at the time.

Music for the Jilted Generation entered the the UK chart at pole position and remained in the top twenty for four months after its release, going gold after only two weeks. It was the most successful dance album of all time and a few months later it was short-listed for the prestigious Mercury Award. Despite it losing out to M People, the guest critics for the television coverage were almost unanimous in their praise for the album, with journalist Miranda Sawyer describing it as 'the only modern sounding album' among the nominees.

Significantly it was *Music for the Jilted Generation* that had brought The Prodigy a wider fan base. Until now the band had been viewed by the mainstream as being little more than ravers, and by this time the rave scene was simply considered to be little more than a joke. People who hadn't been there through the early days would now be writing about it from positions of authority, slagging off the whole movement as being one of stupid druggies whose nights were soundtracked by machine-made music-by-numbers. Although this was true in some cases, it was unfortunate that this became the brush which tarred everyone who had been associated with the scene.

This situation had naturally affected The Prodigy. As their half-empty first UK tour had shown, they had picked up few friends beyond the dance fraternity. Since then they had been making inroads into a more rock-orientated environment, but the transition was still a slow one.

The arrival of the second album was something of a milestone in dance music in that it became one of those albums that it was acceptable to like – no matter what kind of music you were normally into. Admittedly, for a lot of people the album was a small diversion from the norm; nevertheless, its presence in the record collections of disparate people throughout the UK was early proof that the band had a cosmopolitan appeal.

With The Prodigy's careful manoeuvring in order to disassociate themselves from their rave past, the album successfully managed to cross over without taking any of the unnecessary baggage which had dogged their first album. The new Prodigy was more than a rave act. They were an alternative dance band with a rock'n'roll attitude, and people instantly understood this angle.

It was soon after the album's release that The Prodigy flew to Japan for the first time. Invited to play at one of the raves organized annually by Avex Records, when they arrived in Tokyo they were shocked to find that it was actually a mega-corporate fake rave which was also to feature a couple of the most poppy dance acts around at the time, Capella and 2 Unlimited. Such was the band's disgust at 2 Unlimited that they were hardly able to keep their mouths shut, especially after Liam and Maxim had had a few drinks.

'It all started getting a bit messy,' recalls Leah Riches. 'Liam was making all these remarks about them and at the same time one of the band, I think it was Leeroy, was trying to chat up the singer who was actually going out with the bloke in the band.'

'2 Unlimited went up and we were like, "You cunts!" because they're the ultimate description of Euro-shit,' explains Liam. 'We just hated them so much.'

However, at about four in the morning after the show, Liam was lying in his hotel room when suddenly there was a banging on his door so loud that it brought Maxim out to see what was going on as well. In the corridor stood a very drunk member of 2 Unlimited, with a score to settle. As soon as he saw Liam he started shouting, 'Why are you dissing us, man, what's the problem?' Then he saw Maxim.

'Then he goes, "No it's not you, man. It's the white guy." It nearly went off there and then in the corridor.'

It was just one of those situations that inevitably arise when a group of lads on a united mission find themselves faced with the creative enemy; the very people who, to them, represented the selling-out of the dance scene. Only twenty-four hours earlier however and Tokyo had witnessed the gang from Essex in full flow.

The band and crew had been knocking back the tequilas since they'd arrived. When they were suitably drunk they went out for a look around. Once Keith and Liam went into a supermarket, the duo's irrepressible humour came to the fore.

'We just went in there to get something to eat but all of the packets were written in Japanese so we had to open them all to find out what they were,' laughs Liam. 'Then Keith gets it into his head to photocopy his arse. God knows why but he had to do it. So he gets on the machine and realizes that he hasn't got any change so he calls the geezer behind the counter for some change. He came up to us and we just thought "here we go, we're going to get chucked out", but he just put some coins in the machine. He even adjusted it so that Keith could get the best possible picture of his arse. It was mad!'

Soon after the Japan experience, The Prodigy received some bad news; they'd been dropped by Elektra, their American Company. Only a month after *Music for the Jilted Generation* had stormed the charts in Britain and across much of Europe. Ironically Liam had probably done more than enough to help the company in their efforts to break the band in the States, even recording alternative US versions of tracks. Notwithstanding, they still deemed The Prodigy as unlikely to ever achieve any success Stateside and threw them in the wastepaper basket.

'To be honest, I wasn't bothered,' declares Liam. 'I hated the US. We were more into the UK thing and they just couldn't get it. Their idea of dance music was house stuff like Kevin Saunderson.'

So the band continued to promote Britain's biggest dance album ever without a US deal, and released a single from the album called 'Voodoo People'.

In many ways it was 'Voodoo People' which really broke the mould of The Prodigy's singles. It was a hard techno dance track which featured a multitude of samples of 'real' instruments. As such, shuffling snares sat next to a flute which was overlaid by a guitar sample from a Nirvana song. Liam Howlett describes how this track came out of his frustration at the way the scene was going.

'I'd lost the buzz so much that I just had to do something for myself and not with a rave or club in mind. I had to go out of my way as much as I could to make records that didn't have a keyboard sound; using more natural instruments. I sampled a Nirvana track and basically I didn't think a lot of people would like it, but I did; I thought it almost had a 1970s vibe.'

A year later and Nirvana's David Grohl was standing sidestage at Scotland's T in the Park festival, with local television personality Ewan McLeod when the band launched into a blistering version of 'Voodoo People'. Grohl turned to his Scottish host and said, 'That's one of Nirvana's songs they've sampled.' McLeod was amazed that the band had let The Prodigy get away with such an obvious steal but Grohl simply continued, 'They're the best fucking rock'n'roll band in the world man, better than Nirvana ever were.'

Later he would meet the band backstage where he broached the subject of the sample.

'Dave came in the changing room this time and we obviously knew who he was,' begins Liam. 'Anyway he goes, "I really liked your album, especially where you sampled Nirvana." Leeroy was like going, 'W-w-w-umm-wo,' he was just gobsmacked.'

'He was like some guilty boy being interviewed by the old bill,' adds Keith. 'I was like, "Ask Liam," about it.'

In fact Liam didn't actually sample the guitar riff. Instead he got a guitarist called Lance Riddler to play the part in the studio and from this session came the sample. Amazingly, none of the representatives of Nirvana attempted to get a writing credit on the album. And as for Dave Grohl, he was to become a regular figure dancing in the wings at their gigs; indeed, The Foo Fighters (which Grohl formed after the suicide of Nirvana's frontman, Kurt Cobain) ended up playing support on numerous festivals throughout 1996 and 1997. Furthermore, in an interview with *Melody Maker* in early 1997, Grohl spent almost half of the allocated time with journalist Victoria Segal passionately raving about The Prodigy.

The video for 'Voodoo People' represented a dramatic departure for The Prodigy. Filmed in the equatorial heat of St Lucia in the Caribbean, the action for the promo was based around the band being chased by a witchdoctor played by Leeroy. Including many scenes of real voodoo magic and some distressing scenes of people under spells, and in trances etc, 'Voodoo People' also had an incredible amount of humour in it. Leeroy had his face painted half black and half white. Maxim was featured driving at breakneck speed, but always through the same bit of jungle, while Liam was shown running at the jeep, shirt open, slightly flabby chest bouncing in slow motion like the introduction to *Baywatch*. The video climaxed with a suitcase being thrown down a steep hill, from which stepped a dazed Keith Flint (who has already been strung upside down from a tree at the beginning of the video). In direct contrast to the '(No Good) Start the Dance' video, this one was filmed in colour and made far less of an attempt to capture the individual personalities of the band.

'Voodoo People' followed all the previous singles into the upper reaches of the charts, and also introduced a host of new fans to the band. Not surprisingly these new kids had largely come over from the grunge camp. A fact which became painfully obvious when the band stepped out on their next UK tour. The ponytails and shaved heads of rave had now been infiltrated by the dreadlocks and tangled hair of the alternative kids. And, to the embarrassment of Leeroy, the audience also boasted a number of people with their faces painted black and white as per the 'Voodoo People' video. The Prodigy's gigs would never be the same again – in fact they just got better.

*   *   *   *   *

It starts like the greatest rock'n'roll gig you've ever seen, Keith rolling on in a perspex Gladiator ball, the crowd getting cooked stellar. What makes The Prodigy so great is the superb variety. Behind his wall of decks, Liam takes on a whole trunk of sound and seemingly can turn his hand to anything. Like Tim Simonon and Tricky he is that rare thing – a master electrician who doesn't let any edge evaporate in the mix. He understands music deeply and plays up to the best in every genre, before slamming it all together in one perfect, spine-shaking sonic hit. The Prodigy aren't a Sweet for the 1990s, they're a Stooges. The blast is primal, the life-swallowing beats that vital. Gig of the year so far? Oh yes.

Neil Kulkarni, Melody Maker

Where most bands would have sat back after such a successful album, The Prodigy decided to take their show on the road once more. This time the increased theatricality of their videos came through in the band's performances. The increased exposure to rock bands they had experienced on their European festival gigs had provided them with a greater insight into the workings of the gig circuit over the rave scene.

With rave, the performance was only a part of the whole event. With a gig however, personalities were paramount. The Prodigy had already started to push their live shows further down the road marked rock'n'roll but only now did they take their show towards the visual extravaganza.

Keith would come on stage in a straightjacket, struggling for freedom while Maxim proceeded to smash fake glass bottles over his head. Alternatively, Keith's entrance would be in a huge inflatable hamster ball, in which he would roll across the stage until he finally fought his way out. The show became pure performance as Keith's previous ravy smiles were finally dispensed with and replaced by the look of the deranged. To see his heavily sweating face leering towards you, eyes accentuated by dark make-up, hair stuck to three days of stubble, was like meeting Freddie Kruger and Charles Manson rolled into one and given the keys to the asylum.

Meanwhile Maxim adopted wilder outfits, a metal gauntlet and a collection of weird, otherworldly contact lenses. His act had developed from the menacing MC with one hundred per cent street suss into the microphone-wielding rabble rouser, standing on the edge of reality, flicking his tongue like a snake who has just tasted the scent of his first kill in days.

'I like to get on people's nerves, I like to fuck with people's heads,' reveals Maxim. 'Whether that's people in the crowd, the sound and the lighting crew, the security – I just like to fuck with them all. People come to our gigs and they just think I'm doing my job and then I start on them and they don't know how to cope with it. It's probably a form of bullying, maybe I was bullied at school and I'm getting my own back! Nah, the thing is, I like to give people a show to remember. I love the idea of someone coming to the show and afterwards telling his mates, "Fucking hell I was down the front and Maxim came up to me and completely freaked me out." It's something that you wouldn't forget.'

As Keith and Maxim took their stage image further, Leeroy continued to maintain his B-boy style. His height and unique dancing style already lent him an air of theatricality and ever since the embarrassment of the green and white costumes he'd vowed never to dress up again.

'It's just not me, is it?' he explains. 'I was never into costumes so I'm not going to dress up like a clown or whatever now. I wouldn't even join the scouts when I was younger because I just wasn't into the uniform. With me what you see is what you get.'

The stage set too became more extreme. Liam's gear was housed in a metal frame, while above him hung a screen which flashed a succession of computer-generated images interspersed with shots of the band. The result was an audio visual powerhouse which forced people to take note.

Another development was the introduction of a guitarist for tracks like 'Voodoo People' and 'Poison'. The six-string addition added a rockier dimension to the band and it also enabled those people who still argued that sampled music wasn't real and that therefore it wasn't really live, a way to hook onto the band.

Perhaps more significantly, the band were now only playing in traditional rock venues. Their dates in Europe tended to be on the same bill as rock bands. The days of the rave PA were long gone; The Prodigy had developed into the best rock'n'roll band in Britain.

Throughout 1994 and early 1995 the band toured constantly. Barely a night went by when The Prodigy weren't playing somewhere in the world. Indeed it was through this constant gigging that the band managed to continue building up a world-wide following.

In March 1995 the band released a new version of 'Poison', their fourth single from *Music for the Jilted Generation*. The slowest track

that Liam had written since he discovered the free parties at the end of
the last decade, it not only echoed his hip hop past but also hinted at the
direction he was heading in. It was also notable for the fact that Maxim
now had a full vocal on a track.

'I worked for a long time on that vocal line,' explains Maxim. 'It was
all about the rhythm and ambiguity of the words. It was actually quite
hard to do because I wanted it to say something. Without saying too
much.'

The finished hook-line was simple but effective. *I've got the poison,
I've got the remedy. I've got the poison, the rhythmical remedy. I've got
the pressure, the pressure.'* Liam explains why the lyric worked so well:

'I think it works really well, on two levels. In a basic, immediate
way, it's a good hook-line about, well, poison. But if you look deeper it
could be about drugs or anything that might be represented by poison. I
think that's the way the music works too. On the one level you have this
simple, direct stuff which is really immediate, but listen harder and
there's all this weird stuff going on too.'

The single was backed by three other versions of the track, including
a thrash-guitar, heavy mix called 'Rat Poison' which was perhaps a
blueprint for what was to come.

*   *   *   *   *

**Glastonbury, June 1995. It's getting dark, and a field in front of the
NME stage is heaving from front to back as searchlights sweep the
crowd and discordant samples echo through the air. Maxim strides to
the edge of the stage, and stares into the night with crazy white eyes.
He raises his microphone. 'Glastonbury . . . Are you ready to rock?' As
the shattered glass breakbeats of 'Break and Enter' ring out at huge
volume and thousands of dancing people become one enormous
moshpit, the crowd are greeted by the deranged spectacle of a flame-
haired Keith Flint rolling onto the stage in a massive glass ball. There
was no more room for doubt – The Prodigy's state-of-the-art fusion of
dance energy, rock power and visual madness had arrived.**

Chris Sharpe (XL Records press officer), press release, May 1997

Throughout the summer of 1995 The Prodigy played the festival circuit
with a passion. They had a message to get across and they were going to
do it through sheer hard work. In May they played at the first Tribal

Gathering, a dance festival which the band were pleased to see had attempted to stay true to the original free party vibe. Keith had cut off his long locks for the occasion and in their place he sported a short, orange spiky look. It was the beginning of his transformation into the electronic punk that their video collection had already claimed him to be. Unfortunately, the set was marred by a lunatic stage diver smashing up a load of equipment, forcing the band to cut their set short. However the biggest gig of their careers was to take place just over a month later – Glastonbury Festival.

Glastonbury, the Rolls Royce of festivals throughout the world represented for many bands, the ultimate ambition. For The Prodigy it was more than merely an ambition. It was essential if the band were to reach the wide range of people they thought that they should be getting to. In many circles the band were still written off as merely a rave band and, despite their success, some quarters of the press still refused to treat them with the kind of respect that would be awarded to Brit pop bands like Blur.

One of the problems lay in the fact that the dance explosion of the early 1990s had practically obliterated the indie guitar scene. Indeed, with bands like The Happy Mondays and Primal Scream introducing dance rhythms, dub and club mixes to their sound, it seemed, to those who didn't understand dance music, that the effects of Ecstasy were getting everywhere.

Another problem was that the dance scene was an independent, underground industry and, as such, it operated in a different way to the major labels. Experience had shown the majors that the biggest hits of the time came from independent labels and as soon as the majors even attempted to muscle in the ravers lost interest in the track. Indeed, The Prodigy's early success may not have been achieved had it not been for the fact that people would collect a label's output, and XL Records were a very collectible label. Furthermore, had 'Charly' come out on a major it would have all but disappeared. After all, even though the mainstream celebrated the A-side, it was 'Your Love' on the flip-side that the underground bought the record for.

'Only yesterday someone came up to me and said that "Your Love" was still our best tune,' says Leeroy at V97. 'But it was massive. A real anthem of the year, far more than "Charly" which the radio got into.'

A third problem with the dance scene lay in its almost dogged refusal to be marketed through traditional means. There were no stars, so the industry couldn't employ the usual star system of promotion to sell records. And DJs just weren't as exciting a prospect as rock'n'roll singers.

Perhaps as a direct reaction to this, the industry and the media conspired to promote retro guitar bands under the banner of Brit pop. On the edge of this scene were Oasis. On the edge because, in reality, they were a law unto themselves. However, as Oasis grew in stature they became adopted as a standard for the anti-dance people. Inadvertently, the industry and media promoted the concept of a dance/indie divide, with dance music instantly relegated to the position of underdog.

It is interesting to note that when The Prodigy were playing to five thousand people in a rave, Oasis were still lucky to pull twenty people in the back room of a pub. As a result, The Prodigy had a great deal of experience of playing to huge crowds, whereas Oasis and their ilk were relative newcomers.

On the night The Prodigy were booked to headline the *NME* stage at Glastonbury and Oasis were scheduled to play the main stage. Unfortunately both bands were due to play at exactly the same time, which instantly set up a Prodigy versus Oasis vibe between the dance heads and the indie kids.

In the event, The Prodigy won the battle hands down. As an almost static Oasis went through the motions of playing their songs and even introduced Take That's Robbie Williams to the crowd, word quickly spread that The Prodigy were rocking the next field. People left in droves to check out the dance troupe. To their surprise, what they found was a high-octane, beats-fuelled machine set for a full-on collision with oblivion. The Prodigy were so alarmingly brilliant as to be almost out of control.

'To watch thousands of Oasis fans trample down five hundred tents to get into our field was a dream come true,' explained Keith to *Blah Blah Blah* magazine some time later.

For Maxim, the Glastonbury experience was to remain his favourite performance ever. Talking some two years later, he exclaims, 'Glastonbury was a total buzz. Just to be there as a dance band at a rock festival was such a buzz. I couldn't even see the crowd but I was so wrapped up in this buzz that I had to get all of this energy out. Sometimes I've got so much energy that I get these head rushes on stage, I go dizzy and I just think, fuck, I'm going too far. It's like I'm doing myself damage. That always happens at the best gigs. I had a lot of head rushes at Glastonbury.'

January 23rd 1992 Liverpool, Mountford Hall – Keith and Leeroy catching flies.

February 1992 – Those green and white rave-jockey costumes!
"I think it's one of the biggest mistakes I've ever made." Liam Howlett.

April 10th 1993 The Astoria, London. Flinty and Maxim get caught up in the crowd.

Mary Scanlon

May 1992 – Boys from the wood. The Essex homies get chilled.

September 17th 1993 Munich. Flinty the tartan terror parks his bum.
Maxim makes like a chair.

1994 – "Lads, I think I've pulled!" Liam plays with his model collection on set for "No Good (Start the Dance)" video

"Nah, I'm telling you she's up for it."

Jamie Fry

"Shit, I had my eye
on her and Liam's
copped a feel already."

. . . and finally.

Melanie Cox

May 24th 1996, Essential Festival, Brighton. "I love it. I'd die for it. It's why I'm here . . .Getting on stage and being able to let off all that energy and have that attitude, it's the ultimate. You're friggin' lawless. Absolutely lawless." Keith Flint

Tom Sheehan

December 1996 – Keith does Begbie from Trainspotting for the Christmas issue of Melody Maker.

Tabatha Fireman

October 18th 1996 – "I love to get at people when I'm on stage. I like to scare the hell out of them so they have an experience they won't quickly forget." Maxim Reality

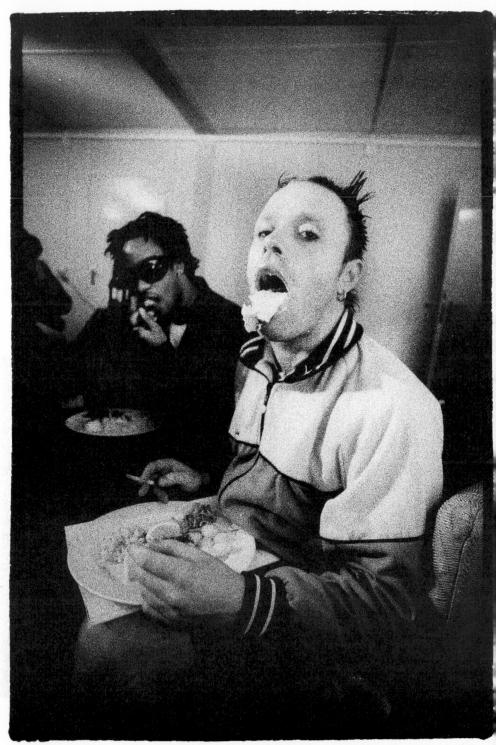

May 1997, Boston – Keith barfs backstage.

May 1997 – "This has got to be the smallest spliff you've ever rolled Leeroy!" Maxim and Leeroy chilling on the tour bus somewhere in America.

May 1997, New York – The Prodigy line up for the Vox cover.

May 1997 – Sniffing the lamp posts in New York.

May 1997, New York – Maxim and Liam meet the stretched heads of the Voodoo Crew.

June 17th 1997, Stanstead Airport, Essex – "Right that's it, I've just about had enough of your questions. I'm going home." Leeroy gets physical while Maxim hits the pillow.

He wasn't alone, as the entire audience watching them seemed to be overtaken by rushes as well; head, heart and spirit rushes.

A month later, The Prodigy roller-coaster pulled into Scotland for the T in the Park festival. Long since a stronghold for the band, this date was particularly spectacular, as Scottish TV presenter Ewan McLeod recalls, 'I'll never forget the sight when The Prodigy came on stage. All day the crowd had been really quiet, hardly even moving until The Prodigy came on. It was amazing. All of a sudden everyone in the park was going mental and, because it was really hot, all of this dust started to get kicked up. I was watching from the stage and after about ten minutes of the band playing the whole place had been engulfed by this huge cloud of red dust. It was really weird. Then they went on to play an absolutely blinding set.'

The Prodigy summer schedule was going through a particularly frenzied period. The T in the Park event took pace on the Friday night, the following night the band played at Ireland's Feile festival and on the Sunday they appeared at Iceland's Uxi festival. In order to cope with the travel problems that this created the band resorted to hiring a private plane – by now one of the band's favourite indulgences when they had a particularly difficult itinerary. Not because they were loving the rock-star lifestyle, nor was it because they didn't like travelling with the common people any more; the main reason was that it gave the band a chance to fly the plane. On these little trips it had become common for one of them to take the controls from the captain. Keith particularly was up for it, such was his passion for big machines. But then, all of the band has a healthy interest in fast, powerful cars, and what better than the full power of an aeroplane at your fingertips?

In October 1995, a short burst of UK dates was announced. Of these the most notable was on the 28th, at Ilford Island in Essex. Not only did this represent a kind of homecoming gig, since it was on their home turf of Essex, but it also transpired to be the date that Keith chose to reveal his new ultra-punk style. His hair had been shaved down the middle, leaving two multi-coloured horns. Furthermore, his body, like the rest of the band's, was heavily pierced. Nose rings, tongue studs and tattoos were the order of the day.

Ilford Island was also memorable for being the first time the band played their forthcoming single. Scheduled for release in January 1996, the track was a slow and heavy breakbeat number with guitars liberally splattered all over it. It also featured Keith's debut vocal performance.

That track was 'Firestarter'. Little did the band know that it was to send their lives into orbit. Not that Keith cared, he still had to get over his first-ever job in charge of the microphone.

'That first time I sang on stage, well . . . I did a parachute jump a couple of weeks beforehand and the whole scenario of building up to it was petrifying. Singing live for the first time though was even worse,' admits the self-confessed adrenaline junky Keith. 'It was like, "fucking 'ell." I've been out there, done my thing, people didn't chuck shit at me so I know it's going down all right, but now I've got to open my mouth. I know the track sounds good and I don't want to let anyone down with shitty vocals. I was completely terrified. The whole gig didn't seem natural. Normally when I'm on stage there's nothing in my head and this night there was this voice going "Firestarter, Firestarter" over and over again. Here's me, I've been smoking weed for days, I'm thinking "shit, my memory's going to give out, the worst shit's going to happen". It's like being in the school play and it coming to your bit and you freeze. I tell you what, that whole gig was worse than that parachute jump.'

Keith completed the task with honours and the band returned home so that Liam could get on with recording new tracks. If the recently debuted 'Firestarter' was anything to go by, the new album was going to be an incendiary device of epic proportions. The only problem was that Liam hadn't written much of it yet. In fact he'd hardly put finger to keyboard. As with the second album, Liam had once again spent his time putting his feet into a snowboard, on what was to become his annual pilgrimage to Colorado with Keith and Leeroy.

In December the snowboarding had to stop, as more gigs loomed on the horizon. For the first time in their career they were to play in Russia. It was a country that had never really attracted any of the band, but *Music for the Jilted Generation* had sold over 200,000 copies over there so if the fans wanted them, then the fans would get them. Unfortunately it proved to be an awful gig with people just standing, staring at them; never smiling at all.

'I tell you what, the whole place was weird,' expounds Leeroy. 'Trying to get out [of Russia] was the strangest, literally took us about three hours to get a hundred yards in the queue. We had this group of English schoolgirls in front of us, all about fifteen and that. There were nine or ten of us and we all started to get a bit angry so it got to a point where it had to turn into humour or it would have got a bit awkward. So we started taking the piss out of these girls. Then we started on our guitarist of the time, his name was Jim and he was really white. No, I mean it, really fucking pale. Anyway it was nearly Christmas so we started singing these carols but we replaced all of the words with "Jim". It was like, "I'm dreaming of a white . . . JIM!" and things like that. It was stupid but we all thought it was funny. So we were all pissing ourselves laughing and then I kind of dropped back to watch what was going on. It was amazing to see how everyone was trying everything to edge ahead of the person next to him, even through we were all mates. Eventually we got to passport control, and they were opening the bags; there was a geezer with a mirror checking under our coats. It was really full-on. So we vowed we'd never go there again.'

It was a vow which was to last exactly two years, as the band returns to play the Red Square in October 1997.

FOUR
Burning Down the House

I love it, I'd die for it. It's my life, it's why I'm here. You know when you've gone through those stages of saying, 'Why am I here, why am I going through all of this shit just to get this shit?' I feel like now I can say, 'Yeah, this is my boat, this is why I'm here.' And I'm just going to make the most of it and soak it all up like a sponge. Getting on that stage and just being able to let off all that energy and have that attitude, it's the ultimate. You're friggin' lawless. Absolutely lawless.

Keith, June 1997

It's a good thing that somebody like Keith was thrown into the limelight because it lets people like him (like me), somewhat expressing their individuality with bright hair and piercings, get a bit more respect than before any firestarting episode. There are still a few who need to be Prodigally educated though; mainly kids in 'Kappa' tracksuits who listen to happy hardcore, claiming they are normal (?!) and shouting 'Firestarter, oi Firestarter' at me as I walk down the street, which I find quite amusing. It's not because I listen to The Prodigy, it's not because I make it obvious I like The Prodigy, it's the image thing you get the stick for. But I'm complimented (even though I'm female) because The Prodigy are a bunch of fine young men.

Kristie Woods, Prodigy fan, Midlothian, Scotland

A disused tube tunnel near Aldwych underground station, deep below the streets of London. A smoke machine belches out fumes as a camera crew focus on Keith. He's dressed in a stars and stripes jumper, a heavy chain hangs around his neck and his eyes are circled in thick, panda-black make up. His hair is jelled into the customary side wings, while the middle has grown to a number one shave. Thanks to heavy back lighting and stark illumination on his face, he looks startling. More frightening than any other version of Keith previously seen on stage.

As the backing track rolls he adopts a stance which makes him look like an evil puppet; his hands hanging loosely by his side, his body leaning slightly to one side. He is a marionette, a possessed Pinocchio, whose internal strings are slowly tightening with the music. Suddenly he erupts in a series of jerky, fit-like movements. His face snarling into the camera he spits out the opening lines to the song: *'I'm the firestartahhh, the twisted firestartahhh.'* Rock'n'roll history is in the making.

Seeing him on TV, children all over the country run and hide behind sofas; the evil black and white image of a man has, it would seem, terrified the nation's pre-teens. Not only that, but the song has also encouraged young people to become arsonists. At least, that's how the nation's tabloid press reacted to the video of 'Firestarter' on *Top of the Pops*. And, acting as the voice of the silent majority, they swung into action in an attempt to ban this epitome of evil. 'Ban this Evil Record' shouted the news-stands the next day. 'Save our Children from the Rock Star from Hell.'

With three minutes and forty-five seconds of sneering attitude, dirty hip hop and leering electronic funk, The Prodigy had reintroduced the generation gap into the living room. Suddenly everyone had an opinion about Keith Flint, 'that Prodigy geezer'. For the dancer-turned-singer there was an irony in the situation. Having long experimented with the punk image, he'd finally followed in The Sex Pistols' footsteps and felt the wrath of the tabloid press. In 1977 the Pistols may have caused people to put their booted feet through television sets after a bout of swearing on Bill Grundy's *Today* show, but nineteen years later Keith was getting the same reaction simply because of the way he performed, and those 'Firestarter, punking instigator' lyrics of his.

Filming the video for the single back in January 1996, the band could hardly have realized how it was going to send them on a trajectory marked interstellar. If they'd known that then, perhaps their underground attitudes would have taken over and the video been abandoned. After all, they'd already scrapped one video for the track for being too commercial and not capturing the vibe of 'Firestarter'.

'It was in black and white and shot in one cheap location but "Firestarter" ended up being the most expensive video we ever did, simply because we did it twice,' laughs Liam. 'When I watched the original I was just like, "No way, this isn't us." They'd made this really tacky film, with loads of obvious references and that. It just didn't represent us as people at all. It had to go.'

So Walter Stern was called in. Stern had been the man responsible for both the 'Poison' and '(No Good) Start the Dance' videos, the band's favourite so far, so they felt happy with him back on board.

In an interview in the *Times*, Stern revealed that his main aim was to make a 'visually stunning piece of film that looked menacing, but not mainstream'. A representation of the entire ethos of the band in fact.

However, there was another side to that 'Firestarter' video. With most of the action centred around Keith, and Liam spending a lot of his time behind the camera helping with the directing, both Leeroy and Maxim were left upstairs in a waiting room with nothing to do but relax, play their Sega games and chat. After a few hours of this Leeroy got bored beyond belief and came into the tunnel shouting, 'I'm fucking sick of this, man, I'm going to get a drink.' Which is exactly what he did do. Only he didn't just drink a couple of pints to ward off the boredom, he sank a crate of fifteen bottles, gradually turning from the calm joker into a leery drunkard with a spot of trouble on his mind.

Leeroy returned to the set and stood there, giving the crew a hard time and generally being abusive. Because of the heavy dust the crew were wearing face masks and Leeroy immediately started calling them Altern 8 among other, more insulting, things. And all the while Keith was trying to concentrate on his performance.

'Leeroy was wearing this yellow T-shirt and he was growing his Afro and sideburns at the time. All you could see through the dust and smoke was this yellow shirt appearing all over the place,' laughs Liam. 'Then all you could hear is this mouthing off.'

Of course, when it came to Leeroy's turn to be filmed he was still in no state to perform, but after a number of takes he kept his steps in time and sorted himself out. Yet the shame still remains. To this day, whenever he sees the 'Firestarter' video he just shouts, 'Who's that twat in the yellow shirt and Afro? He's bang out of order.' Unfortunately for Leeroy he would be seeing a lot of that twat in the yellow shirt and Afro. Because, for the next few months 'Firestarter' was everywhere.

As a track, 'Firestarter' was a natural progression from 'Voodoo People' and 'Poison'. It featured a huge guitar sample lifted from The Breeders' 'SOS' along with a small 'hey, hey, hey' lifted from an old Art of Noise track, for which Liam had to pay heavily. When these disparate parts were added to the huge and loping breakbeat and sneering, siren-esque keyboard refrain the collective sound was awesome. With the addition of Keith's cyber-punk growls, however, 'Firestarter' turned into one of those instantly memorable tracks which haunt your sub-conscious from daybreak to sundown.

For Keith, the cathartic experience of singing for the first time was like nothing else he'd ever experienced. For years he'd been expressing himself on stage with moves, when suddenly Liam had given him a new way of expressing himself; Liam had given him a voice.

'I remember playing the track to Keith and him saying he wouldn't mind having a go at some vocals for it,' says Liam. However it's fair to say that Liam himself wasn't all that excited by the idea. After all he'd heard Keith singing along to U2 tracks in the band's tour bus and his wasn't the voice you would describe as 'classic'. Nevertheless, Liam respected Keith enough to know that he must have a pretty strong idea to have mentioned it, so he agreed to try it out.

Later that week they went into The Strongroom in London, where Liam always recorded the vocal parts, and let Keith rip. Liam gave his mate enough space to express himself. From the first moment that Keith opened his mouth, Liam knew there was potential for a great track here. Liam's rushing breakbeat-addled techno versus Keith's cider-drenched, ganja-choked punky tones somehow connected in a way that was unimaginable.

Driving back to Braintree that night the duo listened to the track over and over again. Neither of them could quite believe what they'd just achieved. It was so much more than just another Prodigy track. For Keith it was a total expression of his sense of inner turmoil. Here was this gentle geezer from Braintree who liked nothing more than pottering around in his garden, listening to Pink Floyd on his headphones. But here was also a guy whose lust for adrenalin saw him pushing things to way beyond the pale, with his motorbike-riding habits and taste for dangerous sports. An incredible amount of tension had built up in Keith over the years. Throughout his childhood he'd been unable to express fully the frustrations he felt, while also discovering the same problem in completely giving in to the joys of life.

Through his involvement with The Prodigy, Keith had been able to explore certain aspects of his own psyche by regularly forcing himself into new situations. Singing, however, gave Keith a unique chance to verbalize this pent-up energy that had dogged him since his childhood.

'When I was very, very small – eight, nine, ten, when tunes stirred me up more than anything else – I wanted to smack my head on the wall,' he explained to Vox's Angus Batey. 'I really wanted to hit my head on the wall and run at the wall and stuff. I just couldn't . . . get it . . . out. And that's what's happening now. I know the kid is coming out now. That's why doing vocals is so cool, because it's another way out. And that's why I think it's so honest in a way, because I can relate that to something no-one used to see. People used to hear it, and someone used to have to clear up afterwards, but no-one used to see that. I don't think people realize how honest it is.'

The lyrics to 'Firestarter' were far more a part of this absolute naked honesty than merely a series of incendiary statements aimed at encouraging kids into a life of arson. 'I'm the bitch you hated, filth infatuated' found Keith exploring some of the most painful aspects of his own childhood, while also exposing a sense of self-loathing, visible in his hyperactive energy. This energy may always have brought him an incredible feeling of joy inside, but it also brought him endless trouble as a child. Subsequently, the feelings of shame he felt every time he was chastised by his father or his teachers have projected themselves onto the unbridled thrill he feels now as he explores the extreme sides of his nature.

It's an emotional state which gives him an incredible inner strength, while also adding certain twists to Keith's huge stomach tattoo which bears the legend 'Inflicted'. But inflicted by what? According to 'Firestarter' he's self-inflicted.

'That lyric is just Keith – spot on,' explains Liam. 'You know people meet him and think he's kind of on one level, you know this geezer who jokes around and acts like he does on stage, but he's so much deeper than that. I know him well now. I've seen the different sides to him and there's a lot going on in his head. Those lyrics were just such a powerful statement which works on a far more intelligent level than just about starting sodding fires.'

When 'Firestarter' was eventually released in March 1996, some two months late, it was an immediate success. It went straight in at the number one slot, selling in excess of one million copies during its four-week reign. Suddenly everyone wanted a slice of the Prodigy pie. The entire media buzzed with the idea of the band, with everyone chasing their exclusive interview with them. It was as if The Prodigy had only just arrived. As if they'd never conquered the rave scene, never slaughtered Glastonbury and certainly never had any top-ten hits before.

As the furore burnt on, Liam remained completely oblivious to it all.

The record company would no doubt like to have reported that Liam was hard at work on the now overdue third album. In reality however he was off snowboarding again!

*   *   *   *   *

The two lads looked decidedly suspicious as they approached US customs control. One was in a melange of B-boy cum skate-boy clothing, his hair bleached and spiky, the other was dressed in similar but with his feet firmly ensconced in a pair of Northwave trainers and his nose and tongue pierced with silver bolts. As they walked through customs the officials eyed them up and down. They didn't like what they saw. 'Cheap white trash' one of them whispered under his breath.

Suddenly the dog standing next to the customs officer started barking. It had picked up a scent of something illegal on one of the lads and started straining at the leash, desperately trying to get a taste of whatever it was it could smell. If the dog could have talked it would surely have been shouting 'Marijuana' at the top of its voice. As it was, a bark was all it was capable of.

The customs officers were capable of a whole lot more, however, and as they dragged the lads into a back room, the two just prayed that they hadn't left any residue substance in their bags. They certainly were not stupid enough to take any dope out to the States – not only was it in plentiful supply where they were going, but it would have been a little counter-productive to be deported and banned from the US at this point.

In the room the lads were ordered to place their hands against the walls. The smaller of the two instantly assumed the search position; legs apart, arms straight forward leaning on the wall.

'I see you've been through this before, boy,' sneered a guard.

'Nah mate, I've seen it on TV often enough though.'

For the next hour, the lads were interrogated, searched in every way possible and generally humiliated. Still the guards found nothing. Still the dog barked like a lunatic. In the end, frustrated and increasingly bored the customs officials let the lads go with a warning. 'We'll be watching you, you hear?'

'Yeah, yeah,' replied the lads before they walked off to get a taxi to their destination.

Later, in his hotel room, as Liam looked through his pockets for a phone number, he discovered a full bag of weed. Somehow the guards had missed it totally in their not-so-thorough searches. Suddenly, Liam knew it was going to be a great week and he was already skinning up as he phoned Keith in the next room, before the two of them hit the piste for a quick snowboarding session.

The regular snowboarding excursions had become an essential way of letting off steam. The pressure of writing the new album in between the constant touring was occasionally getting to Liam and, whereas the rest of the band could ease the pressure when they were on stage, Liam had no outlet apart from his music. Quickly his long-held love of speed moved from fast cars to freestyle snowboarding runs down the mountains of Colorado. It was a pastime which the rest of the band had fallen for as well.

'For me it was a really natural thing,' enthuses Leeroy in a private plane somewhere over Europe, in May 1997. 'I'd always been on the sporty side. I play football when I get a chance, I used to go skateboarding and BMX-ing. Actually I've just bought a new BMX but I haven't had a chance to go on it yet.'

Snowboarding quickly turned into the only way the band could reach the same kind of highs they enjoyed while on stage. For Keith, the thrill of it all is essential.

'I wouldn't call myself a snowboarder really,' he admits, 'I just love the buzz of catching a perfect 360 in the air. But when you see these dudes doing it for real . . . man it's like poetry. They're the snowboarders; me, I'm just in it for the buzz.'

Some two years prior to this I had phoned Keith for a quick chat about adrenalin sports. I was about to go snowboarding in Switzerland for a feature in *Muzik*, and decided that a little advice wouldn't go amiss. And at the same time I could get a quote for the article.

'You've just got to go for it, know no fear,' he exclaimed over the distortion of his mobile. 'Don't start panicking when you're picking up speed, I mean, what's the worst thing that's going to happen? A broken arm or leg maybe – no problem. Snowboarding is just a total buzz. Actually I want to try sky surfing next. It's where you jump out of a plane with a board strapped to your feet and you surf the air currents. You know that film *Point Blank*, well, that's what our band's like.'

For Keith, this need for speed goes beyond jumping out of planes, off the sides of mountains or into the moshpit at a gig. One of his greatest passions is his motorbike. Indeed, he even made it into *Motor Cycle News* magazine, surely a first for a member of a chart-topping band? In the article Keith and tour manager John Fairs take their Honda CBR 900 Fireblades on a speed test around Bruntingthorpe test track in Leicestershire. Not to be outdone by his companions, Liam also came along with his newly acquired car, a Chrysler Viper Venom, all £73,000 worth, which got up to 175mph on the home straight. The motorbike duo reached speeds of up to 167mph on their Fireblades much to the delight of Keith.

'I've always been into sports bikes,' he enthused to the *MCN* reporter. 'I used to bomb around Essex terrorizing locals on a Yamaha RD400, and then a Suzuki GS850.'

Not that Keith had stopped bombing around Essex. As Angus Batey explained in *Vox*, Keith thrives on the buzz and in order to reach those highs 'he'll turn to his beloved Fireblade motorbike. And do everything he can to get to the point where he almost crashes.'

'Every now and then you have to do something that's a near-death situation,' Keith told Batey. 'I used to enjoy crashing as much as riding. The slow-motion trip that you get as things are coming towards you and the way your head works under these situations, when you are doing speeds of, like, 180mph . . . I imagine sometimes how my back wheel is spinning at that speed, and kind of look at bridges as they're coming up, and imagine hitting 'em. You can almost imagine how far you would fly if you hit something stationary at that speed. At those speeds your eyes kind of flicker, and what you see is gone as you see it. And that's quite a good little buzz.'

In one of the most revealing articles about the band ever published, Batey also drew from Liam some extremely candid quotes about his fears for Keith's safety when he's on his bike.

'I was on his bike doing 160 down the A12, and I was thinking, "fuck, I'm not going to go much faster than this." I was in the fast lane, and I turned round and there was Keith, going past me at 180. This was in the middle of the day, there was loads of cars around and he passed me about ten inches away from me. He's a nutter on a bike, but he's got good control. But yeah, I do worry about him a lot.'

'Without wanting to sound like an Essex-boy poser, when I'm out on my motorbike people don't want to see Flinty on a nice bike, pipe and all that,' Keith later revealed to me. 'They want to see me on the back wheel. People don't want to see the nicer side, they want the rebel that pulls wheelies. So I give it them. But I'm not like someone who goes out to get attention . . . I don't go down the sea front and pose. No, it's all for me at the end of the day. It's my buzz, and if people see me and go, "Look at Flinty, he's fucking mad," then that's OK.'

With all of this high-speed, adrenalin-inducing activity, The Prodigy increasingly became good copy beyond their music. They were into dangerous sports, fast cars and fast bikes, and best of all they scared little kids and disgusted mums and dads; they were everything that had been missing from the pop charts over the last few years – real rebellious stars. Only The Prodigy still refused to see themselves as stars. Sure they had more money to play with, sure they'd begun to get recognized in the street, but that didn't turn them overnight into cocaine snorting monsters with an endless line of women they could use at will. No, they remained the boys from Braintree and their mate from Peterborough. They were just that bit richer.

Perhaps one of the strangest affects of this increased notoriety was the celebrity status that went with it. Suddenly the band were getting invitations to parties hosted by the world's ultra famous. U2, David Bowie, Madonna – all of them queuing up to be mates with the Prodigy gang. All this attention naturally commanded a higher press profile. It was the band's irrepressible 'Firestarter' that they all wanted. Overnight Keith had turned into an icon and the papers wanted the Keith story. Unwittingly, Keith was quick to deliver.

In an interview with *NME* Keith had talked freely about his feelings on the behaviour of famous pop stars. He suggested that Goldie and Björk, who were a couple at the time, had acted like Michael Jackson and Lisa Marie Presley, during the TV coverage of the 1996 Brits awards. Although Keith protested that he'd been misquoted, Goldie reacted by printing up a T-shirt with a huge picture of Keith's head and bearing the legend 'Cunt Face'. He then wore the shirt at the Essential Music Festival in Brighton. *Mixmag* were quick to print a picture of Goldie in his T-shirt, along with an explanation of what had happened to cause this very public altercation.

Soon afterwards, I jokingly suggested to both Keith and Goldie in separate conversations that they should fight it out in time-honoured tradition – with a video game like 'Doom'. Surprisingly they both laughed at the idea and said it would be cool. Goldie wasn't about to forgive Keith for 'upsetting his missus', but he could at least splatter him all over the shop in his favourite game. Keith, on the other hand, laughed it off. He was in a hurry to get backstage at one of the band's festival shows and was already utterly sick of all the attention which surrounded that misquote. 'Yeah, you set it up and I'll do it,' he agreed as he walked out past me.

The following day I walked into *Muzik* magazine to suggest the idea to the editor. Over the course of the next few months the magazine took the idea and ran with it, eventually losing any notion of a video-game showdown, and opting instead for a quiet chat in a hotel with the journalist acting as the referee. The final meeting came together in a massive rush when, after months of wrangling, both parties finally agreed to a date only a very short time beforehand. In fact, in Goldie's case, only on the morning of the proposed meet.

In true showbiz style the two made up, but not before Goldie had taken the opportunity to really push his side of the story, thanks to Keith being late.

'When Keith tried to call me I couldn't talk to him,' moaned Goldie. 'I was livid. I was going to send the boys round his house. I eventually told him to fuck off. I mean, I've got better suits than Michael Jackson. It was so annoying, Grooverider wanted to punch his teeth out. Fabio wanted to knee-cap him. It was total disrespect on his part.'

The duelling couple finally posed together for the cover of the Christmas issue of *Muzik*. Nevertheless, the image of Goldie and his Metalheads posse laying into Keith and the Prodigy lads is a delicious one to savour. The big boys of drum'n'bass versus the fearless four. Chances are the fight wouldn't have gone Goldie's way quite as easily as he thought. Fortunately the meeting never came to blows and hours later Goldie joined French rapper MC Solaar in awarding The Prodigy the MTV award for Best Dance Act.

Keith later admitted to *Muzik* that the whole event had ruined his year – which is saying something when in the same year the tabloids had had a feeding frenzy on him thanks to the whole 'Firestarter' episode. Keith remained philosophical about it all, however. 'They just want a story to sell their papers.'

Yet the interest wasn't to calm down. By mid 1997 Keith had become an object of fascination to many people. The 'Keith look' had become the stock-in-trade of Saturday night pissheads doing *Stars in Their Eyes* karaoke. Pubs from Newcastle's Big Market to London's Covent Garden Brasseries echoed to the sound of people shouting 'I'm a Firestartahh, twisted firestartahhhh'. Furthermore, even children had started to copy his style and hold him up as a hero. Things had come on a long way in the few months since *that* record had come out. In one case a two-and-a-half-year-old girl had developed a deep fascination with the man. She'd put posters all over her walls and refused to go to bed without kissing them first. Eventually, Channel 4's morning chat show *Big Breakfast* invited the little girl on and awarded her with the 'Essential Keith Kit' consisting of tins of green and red coloured hairspray, nose rings, black make-up, chains and an American flag top. They even went as far so to dress her up as Keith.

The 'Keith look' had certainly embedded itself in the nation's consciousness. He truly was that rare thing, a cultural icon. His image will forever represent the late 1990s. However, if kiddy Keith look-a-likes were a strange thing to see, imagine how Keith must have felt when he saw an advert for Lucozade featuring a parody of himself. In the advert, one taste of the drink turns a geriatric wrinkly into a firestartin' Keith-a-like. Keith was slightly bemused by the whole affair.

'I must admit I had the hump when I first heard about the advert,' he exclaims, eyes fixed directly on me. 'I was thinking "don't water me down". My main worry is that people would think I'm endorsing Lucozade. You know, people might think that I'd done a deal and said, "Yeah, use my image but I won't be there." One bloke even thought it was me with make-up on. If people think I'm endorsing Lucozade and then turn their backs on The Prodigy, you know saying, "Look at Flinty just using his success," I'd be gutted.'

Keith's rising popularity was starting to cause him a certain amount of distress. For Keith, his place was as a part of a team, but now people were trying to elevate him as the band's main man.

'It worries me that people might start to look at *me* as The Prodigy when we are four,' acknowledges Keith. 'If I didn't know where I stood with the other guys I think it may become a problem, but I know that we are a unit. Ever since we started the band we've always said there's four of us, not just one. I mean, when people want a picture of just one of us these days we just say, "If you was a car magazine and you was doing a feature on a fucking Merc, would you put one of the wheel arches on or would you put the whole car on there?" Of course you know what photographers are like. They'll go, "Fucking hell, we've got a leery one here with coloured hair, let's stick him at the front."'

Keith clearly had to do a lot of soulsearching to deal with this new pressure. As Leeroy explains, it only made him a stronger person.

'It must be really hard for Keith to have people shouting, "Oi, Firestarter" everywhere he goes. We could be walking through an airport at six in the morning, up all night travelling and there'll be shouts from across the hall, "Firestarter, oi firestarter." Then he'll get inundated with autograph hunters. When you're knackered it's the last thing you need, but Keith just accepts it and takes it in his stride. When we first met, Keith was what you would describe as an under-achiever. He never seemed to have the confidence to go all the way with something. But through all of this he's just become so strong.'

Luckily Keith's support system was all around him. The Prodigy were still very much a four-piece, a gang – despite the outside pressures. However, in many ways the strain of the added tension was beginning to show. With the press following his every move, Keith became more suspicious of people's motives. Being singled out from the band made him feel uncomfortable, as The Prodigy had always maintained a strong group identity and had never promoted one personality over the other. It was one of the things which made the band so special.

Talking to *Time Out* immediately after the success of 'Firestarter' Keith explained just how much the new-found fame had changed his life.

'We can handle it, but no-one else can. Suddenly people aren't capable of giving me back my change in a shop without turning it into a juggling act. Everyone comes into my mum at work and they're like, "I bet he's rich now, then." That's the most disgusting thing anyone can say to you. There's no privacy. "How much did you pay for your car?" Fuck off! Mind you, it helps with the girls because they think they know you so they'll jump into bed with you.

'If matey goes "nice one", that's cool. We appreciate more than anyone else the people who come and see us. People stopping me and going, "Aren't you that fire-eater geezer?" and I'm like, "Sorry, I don't do tricks." There are times when matey goes, "Can you give my girl-friend a kiss?" and you just want to spank his forehead.'

However, Keith's increased visual prescence was to become one of the reasons for the band's success as they once again took on America in 1997. With an apparent lead singer, if only on the video for one song, the American media and public were suddenly able to understand The Prodigy on their own rock-friendly terms.

*　　*　　*　　*　　*

It's July 1996, and a highly excited Leeroy runs into the foyer of a Paris hotel. 'Fuck me,' he shouts, 'be careful when you're going up them stairs. I just got attacked by this fucking dog!'

The hotel is one of the oldest in Paris. More of a guesthouse really, there's barely enough room for two people to pass on the stairs. And as for the lights along the landing? There aren't any.

With the dog in mind, photographer Pat Pope, who was to eventually provide photos for the band's third album, *The Fat of the Land*, carefully walks up the stairs. His arms are full of expensive camera gear and the thought of being attacked by a mangy mutt makes him cling to his bags for some kind of protection. At the top of the stairs he looks along the hallway. It's pitch black and his room is at the end of the corridor. He carefully starts the walk to his room, each step deliberately careful for fear of waking the sleeping dog. Past one door, two doors, three . . . then a floorboard creaks under his foot. His heart starts pumping blood with renewed vigour, he can hear the beat in his ears. But no dog.

A few more steps to the fifth room and he only has one to go. He's beginning to calm down now. Nearly home and there is still no sign of his canine friend. One more step and suddenly 'GRRRWOOF'; he feels the animal attacking his ankles and lets out a scream which nearly wakes the whole of Paris.

'He screamed like a girl!' shouts Leeroy as he rolls around the floor in total hysterics. His plan had been absolute perfection. But not even he could have expected such a great response from his victim as he grabbed the helpless photographer's ankles.

Pat Pope had unwittingly just joined a growing club called the 'I've-been-caught-out-by-Leeroy gang'. For the lanky dancer, these kind of tricks are essential for his state of mind. He needs them just to alleviate the boredom between gigs.

By the summer of 1996 The Prodigy are ensconced in the European festival circuit. An endless trail of huge field after huge field with largely the same corporate rock line-up. Not the most inspiring set of dates the band have ever done, but essential for breaking into the European market. At least in the eyes of the record company. To The Prodigy, breaking anywhere is a complete anathema. All they're interested in is the buzz of being on stage.

However, due to the continued presence of 'Firestarter', many of the festival dates prove to be a great success. The band start to notice a different kind of fan emerging in Europe. Following the pattern set in

Britain, the crowds are less made up of ravers, and come more from the student and rock scenes – a fact that pleases the band immensely. Since they played that last rave at Scotland's Resurrection their dislike for the 'rave' tag has become intense. Indeed, when I suggest to Keith a year later that he's just a dodgy old raver (albeit in fun) the glare he shoots at me could kill an elephant at a distance of a hundred yards. Thankfully I'm a little more thick-skinned.

'That whole rave thing, it's just crap,' he snarls. 'You know, we were about climbing over fences and breaking into warehouses to have a party. We were about driving in convoys of cars to take over a plot of land for the night. What we were about was rebellion, not some poxy kids waving lightsticks, wrapped up in silver foil and sniffing fucking Vicks nasal spray. We were rebels, real anti-establishment rebels, and that's the real core to the band now. We're complete fucking rebels at heart.'

It's a fact which 'Firestarter' almost screams at you, as does the anarchic stance of the gang who are a law unto themselves, who follow their own rules and don't give a damn who gets in their way. It's an incredibly romantic image which ties right into the main line of people's heroic consciousness. We all love a rebel: James Dean, Clint Eastwood, Johnny Rotten – and now Keith Flint and the rest of The Prodigy.

It was this very rebellious spirit which had Europe in raptures of excitement throughout the summer. In England, at the Brighton Essential All-Dayer the crowd climbed the tent poles of the huge marquee for a better look. What they saw was Keith, Maxim, Leeroy, Liam and guitarist Gizz Butt stampeding through new songs like 'Funky Shit' and 'Smack My Bitch Up', alongside older favourites like 'Poison' and 'Voodoo People'. The rock-hard set turned the marquee suffocatingly hot.

The inclusion of Gizz Butt represented the first time that a guitarist actually seemed to make sense with The Prodigy. Previously, the guitarist, Jim, had seemed to have an entirely different agenda to Liam's and, as such, tended to be at odds with the rest of the music. Gizz, on the other hand, fused with it immediately. Perhaps his punk roots helped. In Liam's music he heard the same kind of energy that he'd heard the first time he witnessed The Sex Pistols and The Clash. Since his background consisted of a series of punk bands including, most famously, The English Dogs, the Peterborough guitarist (whom Maxim had seen back in his old days in Peterborough) brought exactly the right energy to the band. Not only that but he seemed to fit right in – perfectly.

* * * * *

As the live roller-coaster trundled on, the record company were becoming increasingly alarmed at how late the album actually was. Richard Russell, by now the record label's MD, had even started to panic a little.

'Richard used to phone me up in the morning,' laughs Liam, 'and when I answered the phone he would say, "Why aren't you in the studio?" But he was cool. He didn't really hassle me because he knew it would be worth the wait.'

The management also refused to push Liam. In reality, they all knew that he would come up with the goods – it was just *when* that they worried about.

Part of Mike Champion's problem was that he had started fresh negotiations in America concerning a deal for the band. His company, Midi Management, had been representing the band since immediately after 'Charly' and during this time they'd already been dropped by one major in the US. The next deal had to be perfect. And part of these negotiations was a definite delivery date for the album. But Mike was not only a shrewd businessman, he was also a good friend of the band's – which meant that, unlike many managers, he actually had the band's best interests at heart – and so he worked his way round the problem in order to create as much space as possible for Liam to work.

Liam explains, 'I was just blank. I guess I just couldn't see it, what I was after. It was just like one long Groundhog Day so I'd do anything to avoid going in to the studio. One minute it would be Playstation, the next I'm off in my car, and then it would be snowboarding. Usually snowboarding if I could help it.'

While Liam was enduring his endless Groundhog Day of creative blank after creative blank, Mike Champion took the opportunity to shop around elsewhere for a deal. It wasn't necessarily because he'd lost faith in XL Records, it was simply that at this stage in the game it would be helpful to find out what would be available. He later told *Music Week*: 'Having investigated the possibilities we realized what a good deal we already have.

'Control over the band's output and their personal relationships with

XL were the most important factors,' he added. 'We also didn't just want to be another notch on a big corporation's limited roster.'

To solve Liam's continued writer's block it would probably have been advisable for him to take an enforced break, without interruption from press or, for that matter, gigs. But Liam chose to carry on doing bits of press here and there. And the gigging? Well, it never really stopped.

In July 1996 they played at the Phoenix Festival in Stratford-upon-Avon as second headline to David Bowie on the main stage. Unfortunately, it was affected by some of the worst pieces of organizational chaos ever witnessed at a UK festival.

With Glastonbury having been cancelled that year, the demand for tickets for Phoenix (usually one of the most unpopular festivals on the UK circuit) went through the roof. However, the promoter, while boasting of their sell-out days and generally popping open the champagne, forgot to organize the traffic properly. Although normally the reponsibility of the local police, it required huge co-operation from the promoters themselves.

In the end, the unprecedented turn-out meant that thousands of people sat in traffic jams for hours on end, and thousands of fans were unable to get to the site in time to hear The Prodigy play.

Afterwards, people who did see the gig raved about it being one of the best gigs they'd seen. And the televised action from Phoenix did nothing to alter that opinion. Gutted!

But not for long. Soon after the Phoenix fiasco, the band were announced as support to Oasis at their massive open-air extravaganza in Knebworth. For The Prodigy, this personal invite from the biggest guitar band in the world represented a growing number of endorsements from the indie and rock worlds. More to the point, The Prodigy were offering a perfect antidote to the fey warblings of the Brit-pop kids. Significantly for the time, Nicky Wire of The Manic Street Preachers appeared in *Melody Maker* wearing a Prodigy T-shirt, and grunge darlings of the wider media, Smashing Pumpkins, incorporated a version of 'Firestarter' into their set. It was a great honour for Liam, who had grown to love the Pumpkins.

The Knebworth date was outstanding. As one hundred and thirty thousand people chanted along, you could feel the tide was really turning for The Prodigy. When Maxim called, the crowd called back. When he said 'jump!', they all jumped. It was a surreal sight as the speakers, staggered throughout the Knebworth grounds, created a time delay, thus creating a kind of aural Mexican wave, with the jumping flowing in ripples starting at the stage and spreading throughout the crowd.

For many, The Prodigy provided the set of the day. For Leeroy, it provided the finest gig of his career. 'It was one of the best days of my life. I was standing there and all I could think was "fucking hell, that's what an army looks like". One hundred and thirty thousand people, it was a really weird experience. It was amazing.'

Even more amazing was the incontrovertible proof that The Prodigy had crossed over the widest audience imaginable. These days the band could count Brit poppers, hip hoppers, grunge kids, metal heads, indie kids and even the odd old raver among their fans.

They could even count the occasional famous person as well, as Simon Price described in *Melody Maker*, 20 July 1996.

'Airport car park, 4pm. An athletic, naggingly familiar looking man with sculpted Slavic cheekbones clambers aboard the coach.

"Hello," says Ilie Dumitrescu. "We are the Romanian national football team. Can we have your autographs for our children?"'

*   *   *   *   *

Somewhere among the hit machine of The Prodigy's singles output lies an EP that never quite made it. On 29 July 1997, ten white labels of the band's proposed follow up to 'Firestarter' were pressed up. The new single was to be 'Mindfields', a track which was already a regular in the band's live sets. And the promotions department readied themselves to roll into action.

'Mindfields' was a very different affair to 'Firestarter'. In it, a down-tempo breakbeat played host to an almost Arabic-sounding keyboard refrain (a strange echo of 'One Love') with a deep, surging bass sound. It was one of Liam's tracks intended to grow in a series of layers and this one certainly did. But it was the inclusion of Maxim's vocal that really brought the track to life.

Instantly tying the track in with 'Poison', Maxim's lyrics were, as usual, simple yet effective; delivered in his trademark ragga growl meets rock yelp. The Maxim vocal style. *'This is dangerous/ Open up your head feel the shell shock/ This is dangerous/ I walk through mindfields and watch your head rock,'* he growls as the track evolves from a quietly brooding animal into a huge and funky beast, fangs bared and claws out.

The single came with remixes from Liam along with an acidic breakbeat meltdown from Heavenly Social DJ Jon Carter, which tied in with Liam's long-held belief that all Prodigy singles should have a blend of styles.

No sooner had the news got out about the single than radio DJs, journalists and industry people started to talk about it. They all knew the track from the live show but the talk was even more authoritative. Everybody had a copy of it. An exclusive of course, or alternatively given personally by Liam. As Chris Sharpe struggled to stay abreast of the gossip, the press hotline became inundated with requests for the single. The Prodigy rumour mill was churning out stories like an old women, out of control and intent on throwing as many gossip bombs as possible. It was to be a limited edition of only 10,000. Liam was fighting against the success of 'Firestarter' and wanted to take things underground again. Liam was under pressure from the record company to come up with another big hit so it *had* to be a vocal track. Liam hadn't actually got any new material so he'd had to put out a track dating back to the *Jilted* sessions. All untrue of course. All just the product of furtive minds.

Then, just as quickly as it had been announced, 'Mindfields' was withdrawn. And, despite the rumours of between fifty and a thousand white labels having been pressed up, the only copy which was actually sent out went straight to Jon Carter because of his remix. As a result, the DJ now owns the most expensive piece of Prodigy wax on the planet. And he probably doesn't even realize it.

Once again the rumours circulated about the withdrawal of the single. In reality it was in no way equal to 'Firestarter' for shock value. In many ways 'Mindfields' did represent a return to The Prodigy of old, which could have seen as being self-defeating for the band, especially as they were now making some headway into America with 'Firestarter'. Yet 'Mindfields' was still incredibly strong as a track.

Among the many suggestions as to why it was withdrawn was one that had Liam close to a nervous breakdown through the pressure of recording the new album. Another simply had it that Liam had just lost his bottle with 'Mindfields'.

'I know there was a lot of shit said about me about it. It was all crap, to be honest. The only reason I kept the single back was because I decided that the follow-on from "Firestarter" had to be stronger. I know "Mindfields" is a good track but it's a slow-building track which isn't direct. I decided that I wanted the next single to have a kick like "Firestarter" without being "Firerstarter part two".'

That kick was provided by 'Breathe'. But the world had to wait until early November for it to appear.

* * * * *

'It's got to have animals in it,' declares Liam to video director Walter Stern. 'Maybe a hippo or something.'

'A hippo!' laughs Keith. 'What kind of noncy animal is a hippo?'

The task at hand: to decide on the format for the video for 'Breathe'. It has to be as dynamic as the sewer shots of mad Keith in 'Firestarter', without returning to old territory.

'I've got this idea to maybe create a scene of tension between Keith and Maxim,' suggests Stern. 'Have them really vibing off each other. Loads of anger, loads of energy.'

'And a wild animal,' interjects Liam.

'But not a fucking hippo,' concludes Keith.

It wasn't unusual for the director to hold long talks with Liam before a shoot. Ever since the débâcle of 'One Love', Liam had vowed to keep a very tight control over the videos for the band. He knew that the visuals of a band are the most direct thing; sight is the most immediate sense so he was determined that what people saw was the closest representation possible of the band. And that meant getting into the individual personalities of himself, Keith, Leeroy and Maxim.

Of course, Liam's own artistic ability was a huge incentive to get involved as well. After all, he'd always helped design the record sleeves and the T-shirts, what was so different with video? As a result, Liam and Walter Stern built up a good creative relationship, and the videos Stern turned out were the band's finest.

'Breathe' itself was no less of a masterpiece than 'Firestarter'. Filmed in full colour, despite the band's dislike of the medium, Stern nevertheless managed to present an incredibly hard and stark image, The dark colours seemed to vibrate, while reds and gold jumped out. Somehow Stern had completely lost the soft colours usually associated with video and conjured up a harsh world of violent technicolour.

The video featured the band in the run-down squalor of condemned apartments, with most of the action centring around Keith and Maxim, antagonizing and singing at each other through a hole in the wall between their respective rooms. Keith, hair dyed purple on one side, green on the other, bolt through his septum and the word 'Inflicted' tattooed across his stomach, leapt around, while Maxim, face and body painted in black tiger stripes, piercing contacts, silver teeth and customary walking stick, played the fearsome devilish overlord.

Meanwhile in adjoining rooms Leeroy looked around, trying to find out where all the noise was coming from, while Liam lay on a filthy old iron bed, sheets stained with years of bodily fluid spillage. The overall picture is disgusting. It's a violent and intense peep into the underworld, with fight sequences aplenty. The conflict between Keith and Maxim was portrayed by fighting cockroaches; Liam's insomnia incessantly displayed by nightmare visions of doppelgangers, breathing walls, shoes flinging themselves at the ceiling and a sink belching bloody water; and Leeroy's pensive inactivity finally stopped by being thrown across the room. It's a superb piece of work which eclipses the 'Firestarter' video with its intensity. And naturally the BBC refused to play it without substantial cuts.

As for the hippo? Well, Liam agreed that it was probably a bad idea. In the end they decided on an alligator. Back in the days of Tarzan movies, the film makers used to replace the huge alligator or crocodile teeth with flimsy rubber versions. Not here though. In this video the band had a ton of man-eating wild alligator, with a full complement of teeth, which was to roam around Liam's apartment. In one scene in the video, the blond-haired sample king can clearly be seen sitting bolt upright in a state of mild terror as the alligator crys its tears under Liam's bed.

'It wasn't that bad,' claims Liam. 'Actually, I'll let you into a secret. They taped its mouth up.'

'Yeah, but that was only after it had taken a chunk out of a chair!' adds Keith. Perhaps the hippo would have been safer. Imagine what the insurance people would have said had anything gone wrong: 'Bitten by an alligator in an old derelict building in north London? You're having us on!'

'Breathe' was every inch the equal of 'Firestarter'. Featuring an almost gothic bass line (which could have been taken from The Sisters of Mercy), it erupts into a huge breakbeat with whiplash industrial sounds cracking throughout. Then comes a vocal interplay between Keith and Maxim. *'Breathe the pressure/ Come play my game I'll test ya,'* invites a leering Keith. *'Psychosomatic, addict insane'* comes Maxim's reply – a hook-line which is to capture the listener's imagination immediately. It would seem that The Prodigy's world was an extremely scary place to live. Whatever had happened to the cat sample and the friendly rave gestures? Lost for good, apparently. Where once The Prodigy's music would urge you to dance, share smiles, grins and water, and generally get on with it, now it simply walks up to you and pushes you in the teeth, kicks you in the groin, takes you by the scruff of the neck and shakes you up and down until you finally succumb to the heavy beats.

Had there been any doubt as to Liam Howlett's ability to equal the anarchic energy of 'Firestarter' then in 'Breathe' he forced his critics to take their words, douse them in dirt and eat them for breakfast, lunch and tea. 'Breathe' went straight into the British national charts at number one, selling in excess of 750,000 copies and thus achieving the platinum status. A first for The Prodigy and far better than 'Firestarter' managed. But the success of 'Breathe' wasn't restricted to Britain. The single hit the number one slot in Iceland, Norway, Hungary, Sweden, Denmark, Finland, Poland, the Czech Republic, and Spain where it spent nine weeks at number one.

The real surprise about the success of 'Breathe' wasn't that its predecessor had set up a particularly hard act to follow, but the simple fact that the new single was all but ignored in the media. The radio only played it on the late-night slots, air time on TV was restricted almost solely to MTV (with *Partyzone* still giving the band more support than anyone), and it was barely mentioned in the press apart from a feature in *The Face* magazine.

The success of The Prodigy was entirely due to the incredibly strong fan base they'd developed through their constant hard work and fierce gigging.

As with all singles, there was another side to both 'Firestarter' and 'Breathe' – the tracks hidden away behind the huge smash hits. 'Firestarter' contained a telling instrumental track which was the equal to anything the band had ever put out. Called 'Molotov Bitch', it continued Liam's obsession with hard breakbeats combined with industrial-fuelled noise. It was immediately huge on the undergound club circuit, with DJs caning the white label alongside The Chemical Brothers and the rest of the big-beat brigade.

The flip-side of 'Breathe' presented an even more telling hint as to the direction Liam might be taking. 'The Trick' was far more hip hop influenced. A slow-building track with a massive funk undertow, its loping grooves and piano flourishes showed Liam to be completely adept at hip hop. In fact, the only thing 'The Trick' lacks is a lyrical twist from one of Liam's favourite rappers – perhaps one of the Wu Tang Clan, or maybe even Ultramagnetic MCs surreal lyricist Kool Keith (aka Dr Octagaon). It was clear that Liam was going back to his B-boy roots. In many ways the catalyst in this hip hop development of The Prodigy came with one of the finest Prodigy tracks not to go under the Prodigy name. The track in question was a remix of 'Release Yo' Delf' by Method Man which had surfaced in April 1995. A superb slice of ultra-phat hip hop, combined with Liam's trademark electronic pulses and wails, the key feature, however, was a continuous, high-pitched, three-note refrain played on the Roland 101. A version of the remix soon made its way into The Prodigy live sets.

* * * * *

On 2 December the band headed out on a British tour. It was the first tour they had played since the exceptional success of 'Breathe', but instead of organizing a couple of shows in large stadiums which they undoubtedly could have done, they decided to play in relatively small venues. Despite their media perception as one of the biggest bands in Britain, they were still trying to stay true to their underground beliefs.

One thing which had whet their appetites for the smaller gig was a party they had played at the Ministry of Sound in London. Not any old party, this one was to launch the new film from the king of the ultra-violent understatement, Quentin Tarantino. *Dusk to Dawn* mayn't have been the usual splatter-fest that the fans of the man had come to expect, but the absolute out-on-the-edge nature of his films meant that only one band could possibly play the party: The Prodigy.

'It just kicked off with a massive intensity,' recalls Leeroy. 'A bit like the old days but even more so, if you get what I mean. Beforehand we'd thought that it would be a bit restrained, because of it being a film industry party, but it absolutely mad – completely in your face.'

Indeed, packed into the Ministry of Sound, the atmosphere was beyond electric. It was virtually impossible to move as everyone hassled to get a place where they could see the band in action. From the youngest film runner to the oldest executive producer, everyone seemed intent on giving the Prodigy show their one hundred per cent, dancing as much as the crush would allow. And the band didn't disappoint, delivering a blistering set of the usual hard and fast mayhem.

The only disappointed people in the place were those who couldn't get into the main space – a huge crowd whose numbers were matched only by the endless queue of people waiting to go to the bathroom, credit card, rolled-up banknote at the ready.

As a direct result of the Tarantino show, and in keeping with their ideals, The Prodigy decided to take DJs Kris Needs and Jon Carter on tour with them in order to vibe up the crowd.

Kris Needs and Jon Carter are well known as party animals in the dance world. Kris Needs had also been known as a party animal in the punk scene and the hip hop world before the 1988 acid house explosion took him by the nose and led him to the twenty-four-hour party people. In the UK dance scene Kris Needs is a legend, and Jon Carter is on his way to achieving that status. To put them together with The Prodigy was asking for trouble.

On more than one occasion, Kris's frightening ability to imbibe huge quantities of alcohol left him crumpled on the floor of one of the band's rooms, or in the hotel foyer, lift, bar – anywhere with a floor became a potential place to lay the proverbial hat. Each new day brought with it the ritual of having to kick Kris's door in to wake him up. Indeed he missed more than a couple of flights over the course of the two weeks. On one occasion Leeroy and Keith had broken into the DJ's room only to find Kris in bed, with Jon Carter cuddled in as tightly as he could get. When the pair of them were awakened, Jon shouted, 'Hey? What's going on?' while Kris merely replied, 'Shit, I was so pissed last night I thought you was my girlfriend.'

It was after Kris had a particularly heavy night with Leeroy that The Prodigy finally got their own back on their tall friend.

Over the course of the the band's existence, Leeroy had become the practical joker among them. With frightening regularity he would dupe the band, friends, visiting journalists and their photographers (especially the photographers) with his highly perfected skills with the old tomfoolery. Whether this sense of humour involved folding over bed sheets, kicking other members of the band out of their rooms during the night or simply sending them on a complete wind-up with stories plucked from his overactive imagination, it just didn't matter. The important thing was that Leeroy had a laugh and the others were just kept with egg on their faces, staring at him with bemused smiles, saying, 'You cunt.'

The band were in the middle of their pre-Christmas British tour and Mr Needs had taken Leeroy on a tour of his favourite shorts. Whisky followed tequila which followed brandy until the two of them could hardly stand. Leeroy's whole body went limp as he started vomiting into nearby plant pots. When the rest of the band saw this they couldn't believe their eyes.

With a look of unadulterated glee, Maxim, Keith and Liam subjected the helpless Leeroy to an endless round of public humiliation. He was almost stripped and sent spinning on his arse across the hotel bar floor. They poured stuff over him, placed plants on his head, shoved cigarettes in his mouth and even broke wind under his very nose. And all the while the oblivious Leeroy just dribbled constantly and occasionally said, 'I need my bed.' Incapable of retaliation, he was totally unable to defend himself, as the band let off the frustration of six years of being caught out by the arch jester of The Prodigy. And, just to add insult to injury, they filmed the whole thing on video. Just as proof of the whole affair. 'Hell, it might even make it into one of our promo videos,' reasoned the persecutors.

Videoing things had become a norm for the band on these tours. It was a way of alleviating the endless boredom of travelling. Earlier on, during the *Experience* tour, they'd initiated a competition to try and capture the most disgusting Polaroid of each other. By this time the Polaroids had been traded in for video recorders and all of the band took every opportunity to capture the others in compromising poses. None came close to the alleged Polaroid of Keith in full flow with two blondes he'd met in Sweden. As the legend has it, Keith had set off with the girls in their car only to be followed an hour later by the band on their bus. As the tour bus drove past a car which had pulled up on the hard shoulder, the band noticed a white bum going nineteen to the dozen on the passenger side. The bum belonged to Keith. The other fine display of limbs belonged to the Swedish girls. The rest of the band were doubtless just a bit jealous.

The video cameras, being less easy to conceal than a Polaroid, had merely turned into objects for the band to act the fool in front of. So each tape would be filled with bare arses, not to mention bare-faced humour and just a little of Keith's endless straight-faced yet hilarious antics. To see Leeroy in such a drunken stupor, however, was the perfect excuse for getting out the video and shouting that immortal phrase 'lights, camera, action'.

The end result was the perfect retaliation, and as Maxim put the camera under his bed that night he smiled to himself, thinking, 'I can't wait to show Leeroy this in the morning.'

The following day Leeroy woke quite late, with a massive hangover. Maxim and the others had already gone down to breakfast, and they were busy recounting the events of the night before to the road crew and just about anyone else who would listen. Arrangements had already been made for a screening at the next hotel that night.

Leeroy, in the meantime, had woken up with a vague recollection of some strange goings on the night before. He instinctively knew that this would somehow have included the video camera and after about ten minutes searching he found the machine, rewound the film and, to his horror, saw what his mates had subjected him to. 'Bastards!' he thought, 'I'll get them back.' So Leeroy took the video, rewound the film, set the camera up in the bathroom and set it to film wall tiles in the place of the previous night's shenanigans.

'Then I was sitting having a crap and thought "oh no, they'll be able to hear me shitting when they play this back". So I hid it in the bathroom cabinet, still filming,' laughs Leeroy. Later Maxim came back to his room and went straight to where he'd left the camera. It was gone, and so had Leeroy. Twenty minutes later he discovered the machine, rewound it and saw Leeroy's handywork. 'Bastard!' shouted Maxim. The evening viewing had to be cancelled; Leeroy had won once more.

Despite such pranks, the tour was an incredible success, but it was on the London dates that the band really excelled themselves. On 22 December 1996, the band pulled up their wagons outside Brixton Academy where they were going to be playing a special Christmas all-nighter. The stage for the event was transformed into the ultimate Prodigy living room with fake leopard skin as the main upholstery feature. The walls were covered with random Prodigy images, like the ant in a circular frame and a picture of a granny with a Molotov cocktail in a guilt frame. A huge cowhide sofa sat on a platform at the back of the stage, while over on the other side you could see the matching armchair. With huge coordinating lightshades suspended from the ceiling and pot plants liberally scattered around, the set was the ultimate in kitsch. The band had taken the theatrics as far as they could go.

'Brixton Academy has to be my favourite gig ever because it had an energy that I could taste,' says Keith with a burst of energy. 'I felt like I was walking through a vibe and a buzz that reminded me of when I went to my first party. The hairs on my neck were standing up and I thought "fucking hell, I can taste it, man". I tell you what, if I could bottle that taste I'd be the richest man alive. Then I might appear in my own advert!'

As Keith testifies, the gig found The Prodigy at their very best. The atmosphere was alive as the band snapped at the synapses, reducing the crowd to a mess of sweat and exhaustion. A feat they repeated on New Year's Eve at Dublin's cavernous venue, The Point. It had been a great year for The Prodigy and they were seeing it out not with a bang, but with a sonically charged nuclear device.

FIVE
Now Play My Game

Electronica is the most exciting thing to have happened for me. Up till now we've just had old grunge bands and people like REM. But that's old people's music. The Prodigy are part of my generation. They're a part of now – not yesterday. Ever since I first saw 'Firestarter' I knew that the band I'd been dreaming of had arrived. And seeing them play in LA was unreal. They're so theatrical and Keith Flint is the most incredible singer I've ever seen.

Monica Bernstein, LA, Prodigy fan since 1996

As 1997 fired up its motors, a strange phenomenon was starting to occur in the US. The sleepy states of the big country were, if the British papers were to be believed, starting to wake up to the joys of dance music. And right in the middle of this so-called 'electronica' explosion? The Prodigy of course. As a result, for the first time in their career it looked as though they might actually conquer America. The irony of this was that it was happening at a time when Liam and the boys had long since given up on the US as a waste of energy.

Late in 1996, the band had actually been offered a support slot which would undoubtedly have assured them of a huge victory stateside. That support was with the massive U2 'Pop Mart' world tour, a travelling event which would surely have brought legions of new fans to The Prodigy's door. But it wasn't part of Liam's agenda. He could see no reason to play the corporate game now, after they'd had such an independent attitude for so long.

'That U2 tour? It's just not what we're about,' dismissed Liam. 'I mean we would have totally broke America with those dates but I felt it just wasn't right for us. Keith really wanted to do it though.'

'Well yeah, it was the excitement of the thought of being involved in this huge machine churning its way round the world,' agreed Keith. 'I was like, "Fuck me, there's got to be an experience there." I mean, take me out of the band, I'm still a person and as my own person I vibe off experience. I really thought that the big machine thing would have been an incredible experience. I wasn't going, "We should have done it 'cos we would have sold, sold, sold." That just doesn't come into my head, I'm not even that clever. I just love the energy – no, I love the fatigue of it all and the U2 challenge would have been amazing. A real gutsy mission to take on the rest of the world.'

But U2 weren't the only people to have come knocking on Liam's door at this time. Not content with dragging in a certain player from the drum'n'bass world to add a spark to his new material, David Bowie also wanted The Prodigy sound. Liam wasn't having any of it. Unlike The Chemical Brothers, who had reportedly turned down the chance of remixing Bowie because he'd invited them out to dinner to discuss the idea and they'd been 'too scared to eat in front of Bowie', Liam just turned him down flat.

'Of course I've got respect for Bowie but I was never a fan,' laughs Liam at the idea that he might one day regret it when he's telling his life story to his grandchildren. 'Keith's into his stuff, but to be honest, to me it seemed like he was skipping along the dance thing hoping to get into the scene. And I just thought "why should I give him our sound just to help his career?" But I know he likes the band because he'd been at a couple of shows dancing in the wings. I spoke to him on the phone and he's really nice but I can't let the fact that I'm flattered by these people, I can't let that emotion affect what I want to do.'

Clearly the reputation of the wild boys from Essex had gone before them, but why should America be shouting their name now? If it was simply because they were being presented as the spearheads for a new movement then none of the band would be happy about it. They'd been separate from any scene for so long. They'd steadfastly built their thing on their own terms and as a result they belonged to no-one. Unlike every other band doing the festival and stadium tour at this time, The Prodigy could truly say that their sound was unique to them. Being lumped in with The Chemical Brothers, Underworld and a whole host of other bands wasn't a particularly good way of being represented.

There were certain aspects which had conspired to create the band's popularity in the States. First and foremost, 'Firestarter' had started to gain a huge amount of air time on MTV, and indeed the band were given daytime showings for the first time in their history. The effect of this couldn't be played down, as suddenly they were being beamed straight into the minds of middle America, where the shock stylings of both

Keith and Maxim grabbed the throats and imaginations of a youth sick to the eye-teeth with the boring AOR grumbling of grunge, REM and yes, U2.

This MTV time had followed positive press reports in the national magazine *Rolling Stone,* which had given The Prodigy a huge thumbs-up for their show in Seattle at the previous summer's EndFest. This major endorsement was followed by an interview with MTV US President Judy McGrath, who sited The Prodigy as an example of 'new forms of music' the channel were intending to pursue in the future.

If the American industry needs anything to wake it from its slumber it's a top dog at MTV; when the President of MTV US says jump, the sleeping dogs not only go into orbit but they will also reach Mars if need be. Suddenly that strange British electronic music that they'd been ignoring for years became huge currency and, in an orgy of telephone numbers, any band with a sampler and a dance beat got that US A&R department call.

Naturally the premier outfits were those that could play live and, as such, The Chemical Brothers, Orbital and, surprisingly, The Orb were the quickest to capitalize. However, most notable was The Prodigy's deal. Not content with any old deal, they hung out for the label which would give them exactly what they wanted. Since the demise of their Elektra contract, the band had been getting records out in the States through a sublicensing deal with Mute Records. As a result they had never seen any great sales in the US. When this sublicensing deal came up for renewal, every major in the country came knocking on the door of Midi Management.

The initial interest was quickly whittled down to just two major players: Interscope and, more interestingly, Madonna's Maverick label. As a part of the Warner corporation, Maverick was able to offer much more powerful inroads into America, which swung the band's decision in Madonna's favour.

In fact, Madonna had also decided on them – soon after the band had signed on the dotted line came a request for Liam to produce tracks for her next album.

'I just told her I was too busy finishing off our album,' states Liam matter of factly. 'To be honest, I think it would have been a huge mistake if I'd have said yes. It would have put the band across in completely the wrong way.'

With this chance to make a bid for success in the States, the last thing Liam needed was to shoot himself in the foot because of the pure vanity of working with one of the most famous women in the world..

'We'll have to put together a plan which involves lots of going to America, because now we've got the level of marketing there that we can tap into,' stated XL press officer Chris Sharpe to *Melody Maker* in their 18 January 1997 issue. 'The promotional infrastructure is already there. You never know, we might sell some records.'

A typically played-down statement, it didn't even hint at the way things were going. But, to be truthful, not even XL Records quite realized just how big things were getting. At this time 'Firestarter' sat at the foot of the US Billboard charts, occupying the ninety-ninth position, but with continued promotion, the single finally cracked the top twenty, selling in excess of 200,000 units.

*   *   *   *   *

Telephone conversation with Liam, February 1997.

MJ: 'Liam, it's Martin.'

Liam: 'Uh. Look I've uh . . . I'm just in from Australia . . . I'm knackered . . . I'll call you back . . . what's it about?'

Shit, I've just called Liam at eleven in the morning, he's just flown across the world and all I need to ask him is about something incredibly trivial. Almost ridiculous really. I've just started a Playstation League in *Muzik* magazine – a complete indulgence for me and the other people involved. It's a strange diversion which has already got Goldie, Massive Attack and Carl Cox, among many others, tapping their thumbs like maniacs, in search of that victory. But now I need The Prodigy's scores!

MJ: 'Look Liam, it's not important, I'll call later.'

Liam: 'No, go on. I'm awake now. I'll be dead to the world later.'

MJ: 'I need your Playstation scores but . . . '

Liam: 'Oh for fuck's sake! I haven't had a chance to play the games yet. Shit, how are the others teams doing? Yeah, listen I'll have the scores for you tomorrow morning. How well did you say Goldie was doing?'

Sure enough when I wake up the following day there's a series of messages on the answerphone. Liam's sorted out the scores, despite his chronic jet lag.

*   *   *   *   *

That trip to Australia was for the travelling show Big Day Out. It was the third time The Prodigy had played the event. Indeed, it was turning into one of the band's most eagerly anticipated jaunts.

Australia had long been into the band. Their albums had sold very well, with *Music for the Jilted Generation* shifting 30,000 while 'Firestarter' had clocked in a total of 25,000 sales. In Australia these kinds of sales are rare indeed, so this particular Prodigy tour was anticipated with a huge amount of excitement.

With them were Rage Against the Machine, Nick Cave, Porno for Pyros and Soundgarden, the latter proving to be a particularly exciting prospect for Keith who had become a huge fan of their stuff. Also on the bill was Bristol lad Tricky, who formed a particularly strong friendship with Maxim over the course of the three weeks.

Most of the tour was staged in agricultural showgrounds so, as Adam Higginbotham reflects in his article in *Select*, 'The result is an event with an unnervingly backwoods flavour, with more of the "you're not frum round here, are yuh, boy?" ambience of *Deliverance* than the pastoral idyll of Glastonbury.'

'I still feel the luckiest man in the world when I'm, like, in Australia sitting on Soundgarden's drink cooler and they're just ten feet away from me,' enthused Keith some months later. 'You know, I'm there with Rage and Bowie and I'm like fucking hell. Then it'll be like "David" (waves) and he goes "Keith" and then you go away and think "fuck, I held it down well but . . . ", you know what I mean? Inside I'm just like this totally excited kid thinking "fuck, that was David fucking Bowie talking to me!" I try not to take all of it home with me though. I try to soak it all in there and then. If you thrived off that kind of shit you'd want to be in amongst it all the time and just get sucked in. But you just have to walk out of it. It may have felt like getting that dream 360 twenty foot up in the air, but hey, I did that in Switzerland and there's no snow here. Know what I'm saying. It's an experience, but you have to step out of it. Can you imagine what it'd be like if I was with me mates and I was going on about me and Dave? It's just not cool.'

During one of the Australian shows the extent to which gigging had become a drug to the band became apparent. Standing backstage, immediately before going on to perform, Liam accidentally put his fingers into the blades of a fan. He thought he'd chopped the end of one of his digits, so bad was the blood flow. The paramedic took a quick look at it and bandaged the wound which, thankfully, wasn't as bad as Liam had at first suspected. He went on stage and couldn't feel a thing as the adrenalin of the situation numbed all pain. The second the gig was over, however, Liam was in excrutiating agony and had to rely on the strongest painkillers available to see him through the following day. Until the next night, when the adrenalin once again worked its magic.

Flying back into Britain, The Prodigy entered a smog of hype. Everyone was now chasing that elusive album. Rumours were circulating, as they always seem to where The Prodigy are concerned, about Liam's state of mind. 'He's on the brink of a nervous breakdown' was the most common suggestion. So how come he managed to get those Playstation scores in?

Liam *was* now feeling the pressure, in fact . So much so that he made a decision which was so against his personality, so against what had gone before, that the band were left completely stunned: 'I decided to miss our snowboarding holiday to Colorado!'

No matter how much Leeroy tried to convince Liam to go with the others for a well-earned break, Liam just kept on declining the offer. He had an album to do, and in the two weeks that they were gone he could probably finish a couple of tracks.

'Two weeks later, Leeroy comes round and goes, "Well, where's all of this new stuff then? Get the DATs on." And I just turned round to him and said, "There ain't nothing." He just couldn't believe it. I'd missed a trip away with the lads for nothing,' says Liam.

Finally having the space that he'd been craving to record tracks, Liam had discovered that he lacked any real motivation for finishing the album. Sure he knew he had to do it, but he couldn't quite get his head into it. But then, once the lads were back on their home turf, coming round to vibe with him, he found that spark again. And he just went for it.

'People find it hard to understand that it's not exactly just a writer's block,' says Liam. 'The biggest problem is that I've got such a clear picture in my head when I'm writing a track, that sometimes it gets in the way. I knew exactly what I wanted for the album, but somehow it just wasn't coming.'

In fact, Liam had already recorded a number of tracks for the album. When he'd first started recording tracks at the end of 1995 he started on the high of a creative burst. In less than two weeks he'd put down the main backbones to 'Firestarter' and 'Breathe' while he'd also finished two tracks in the shape of 'Funky Shit' and, more surprisingly, a cover version of The Specials' 'Ghost Town'. The latter track was in many ways a statement to the band's past, when they'd all been into two-tone and ska before the hip hop revolution of the 1980s. Yet it was soon consigned to the growing shelf marked 'ideas and tracks which will never see the light of day following the release of Tricky's version of the same song'.

Towards the end of 1996, Liam had enjoyed another rush of ideas, and had recorded a series of tracks, including two with guest vocalists: Skin from Skunk Anansie and Crispian Mills from Kula Shaker respectively. The third track completed during this flurry of creativity was with his long-time hero Kool Keith, rapping. It was called 'Diesel Power' and Liam was understandably happy with it.

'To work with Kool Keith, man, it was like . . . shit, I grew up listening to his stuff. I loved The Ultramagnetics, now here he was rapping over one of my tracks. Fucking incredible,' crows Liam, looking like the cat that got the cream and the geezer who scored the winning goal in the World Cup final; he is, to say the very least, a happy man. 'To be honest though, I'm not really that bothered that we dropped "Ghost Town". I think maybe it's a track that's a bit too well known and it's not easy to improve on the original.'

However, Liam had just recorded another cover version for inclusion. Suprisingly it was 'Fuel My Fire', a track by US punks L7. 'Keith came round with the L7 album and loved it. They really captured the rawness of punk rock. I don't think our track is as good as the original but I reckon it provided another angle on it,' explains Liam.

The band as a whole were so fired up about the track that they started to include it in their sets. Nothing unusual about this, since fans of The Prodigy had long got used to hearing new tracks in a live situation first. The only time this didn't happen was when the track had a guest vocalist on it, and 'Fuel My Fire' was mainly Keith Flint – although the recorded version did include backing vocals from Saffron from Republica, who had been a friend of the band's since her days as vocalist in N-Joi.

'We actually thought they were too commercial [then],' admits an embarassed Saffron at T in the Park '97, 'but they were always really good friends. Keith especially has a great personality and what Liam's music has developed into is amazing.'

'Fuel My Fire' was originally played live during the Australian Big Day Out tour as the band's encore. To say the audience were shocked was an understatement. As the surprise of this hyper-punk techno rush sank in, the crowd grew ever more excited, and by the time Keith and Maxim belted out the 'People like you only fuel my fire' chorus, an epidemic of massed pogoing broke out. It was the same story at every gig that followed until the album finally arrived. It was quite a change, for the old end to their sets was based around the *bonhomie* of 'No Good (Start the Dance)'.

Liam explains the reasoning behind the new choice of encore: 'We originally started putting it at the end of our set because I was sick of doing "No Good (Start The Dance)". We always ended on that track, with people from the audience dancing on stage but then we decided that we wanted to do something opposite from that, to really fuck people off. It was like, "Dance to that, you cunts." It was just total antagonism, but then we started to really like that track.'

Some five months later, on 15 June 1997, I am standing sidestage at the band's Paris gig. As the band launch into another blistering run-through of the track, all around me a group of grungy chicks shout like banshees on Hallowe'en. They're L7. This is *their* song. And their reaction to hearing the very first cover version The Prodigy have ever recorded?

Suzie: 'It's totally amazing. It really makes me laugh to hear it, I get choked up a little.'

Gail: 'I am so proud today. I am as proud as a mother. I wasn't even involved in writing that song but I'm still so proud. The Prodigy are awesome and they've really done the track justice. When I heard it I nearly jumped out of my skin. I think we'll do a version of "Firestarter" – maybe. That would sound totally mad on guitars.'

Later I tell the band of L7's suggestion that they should do 'Firestarter'. Their reaction? 'Cool. Yeah, that would be really cool.' There's something of a mutual appreciation society going on here.

* * * * *

A pub in Greenwich, London, May 1997.

'Did you say you had a copy of the Prodigy album, mate?'

The man in the designer leather jacket sitting on the next table had heard enough of my conversation to know the truth. He'd heard me excitedly describing the tracks, dissecting every last detail of the sounds and generally raving about the album for the past hour, to know that I was one of only a small amount of people who actually had a pre-tape of the album. Nothing unusual about that. I'm a journalist, the floorboards of my flat ache under the strain of pre-tapes. It's my job to listen to them.

But this was different. The excitement surrounding this particular album was almost at fever pitch. Ever since 'Firestarter' and 'Breathe' had cracked open the top slots of charts throughout the world, every man, woman and dog seemed to be after that elusive third Prodigy album.

'Any chance that I could come around to your place and listen to it, mate?' the eavesdropper continued, shouting over the noise of the jukebox. 'I'll make it worth your while.'

I was already becoming used to people wanting to hear the album. But actually offering me money? Naturally I became suspicious.

'So why are you so desperate to hear it, mate? Just a fan, are you?'

'Yeah, number one fan. Me an' my missus go all over for them. You at that Phoenix show last year? We were there, down the front. Brilliant it was. That punky geezer, Flinty, he's a nutter, ain't he. Total nutter.'

So the conversation continued, like a jovial game of chess. Each of us trying to suss out the other. Me working out his motives, him trying to work out if I was telling the truth.

A substantial amount of beer later he finally opted to tell me the real reason for his interest. Was he Mr Superfan? Not a bit of it. Joe Smith ('Honest, that's my name, ask anybody . . .') was a representative of that scourge on the music industry, the bootlegger.

'Tell you what, I'll give you five grand up front for it. With more to follow in a couple of weeks. What d'you say?'

Of course the answer was 'No'. But the conversation that followed the offer was a real eye-opener. Mr Smith explained that he could have the album pressed up onto CDs and on sale within twenty-four hours. And then with the extended chain of bootleggers world-wide, it would have been pressed up in every major territory within four days. And the bootleg would sell like the hottest cakes around.

'Tell you what,' he continued, 'The Prodigy outsell everybody on bootleg. Take your Oasis, or whoever. They don't even come close. You know what I mean? I can put a new Prodigy CD on sale in the morning and it'll sell out by the evening. Oasis stuff hangs around forever. Everybody wants a bit of The Prodigy, not just ravers, everybody.'

Even Chris Sharpe, the band's press officer, had come across a similar story. Whilst browsing through a market stall in London's Spitalfields, he came across a CD of the band's gig at the Essential Festival in Brighton, 1996. The guy behind the stall insisted it was one of the best-ever live recordings of the band and was well worth parting with fifteen quid for. Sharpe, on the other hand, had been at that gig. He knew the sound quality wasn't up to much and the resulting recording would be pretty ropy too. He passed up on the offer but only after he'd heard the legend of The Prodigy's popularity.

'The biggest sellers we've got, mate,' said the stall holder. 'Bigger than Oasis, I can tell you.'

In fact the band's popularity among bootleggers was well known to the record label and band alike. Consequently, the few copies of the tape which were sent out came with contracts forbidding the recipient from making copies, or even playing it to anyone else! The most bootleggable band in the world were striking out against the bootleggers.

I never saw Joe Smith again. Naturally annoyed at the loss of a golden opportunity to print money, he went back to his table and left the pub soon after.

'Don't worry, I'll get a copy of it. I usually manage to get everything,' he said, by way of a parting shot.

In the end the stalls of London's subterranean bootlegging trade never did play host to *The Fat of the Land*. That didn't matter though, they still had hundreds of live CDs on sale. The kind of things that only the fans would buy. And The Prodigy have a lot of fans.

* * * * *

The continuous delays on the album had worked in the band's favour. Sure, it was all because Liam had been so stressed out by the pressures of the project, and exhausted from the live schedule, that *The Fat of the Land* had taken far longer to record than anticipated but, as far as the marketing division of the label were concerned, it was perfect.

Owing to the success of 'Firestarter' and 'Breathe', along with the incredible hype surrounding the band's American exposure, everyone wanted a piece of this album. It had generated its own teaser campaign; all the marketing and PR people had to do was capitalize.

On 24 May *Melody Maker* ran with the first interview with Liam about the album. He described 'Fuel My Fire' as 'full-on punk rock, which is going to shock a lot of people'.

'But then that's one of the things about this album,' he continued, 'it covers a huge spectrum, from the home-listening tracks like "Climbatize" and "Narayan" to the full-on tracks like "Serial Thrilla" and "Fuel My Fire". The tracks which are probably closest to what people think of as being Prodigy songs are ones we've been playing live for ages – "Smack My Bitch Up", "Funky Shit" and "Mindfields".'

Of the Kula Shaker guesting track, 'Narayan' (originally titled 'Setting Son' until The Chemical Brothers released a collaboration with Noel Gallagher of Oasis called 'Setting Sons'), Liam stated, 'It was brilliant working with Crispian Mills. We did the main vocal in an hour and then spent about four hours doing the chant at the end of the track.'

He then went on to talk about the Kool Keith track 'Diesel Power'. 'It's a really raw old skool hip hop track with hard electro loops. It really stands out from the rest of the album because it's extremely simple, whereas the other tracks have full song structures.'

Amazingly he announced that he hadn't actually finished the album yet. The final track was to be a Keith Flint track called 'Serial Thrilla', which he had yet to finish mixing. As ever Liam was taking the project to the wire.On 31 May *NME* ran with their own version of the exclusive Liam interview while *Melody Maker* presented a full track listing of the album; complete with description from Chris Sharpe at XL.

The next week *Melody Maker* had a Prodigy-related story in the shape of guitarist Gizz Butt's band, English Dogs, signing to Earache.

On 9 June the first bill posters started to appear around London. At the same time Radio 1, the country's national pop music station, seemed to be playing the band's singles non-stop. By 16 June the entire country seemed to be plastered with posters depicting a crab on a sea shore, claws raised to the camera. With it was the legend '*The Fat of the Land* – The new album by The Prodigy'. Simple, direct and visually arresting. The fever had begun.

By now, every radio station in the country seemed to be running their Prodigy exclusives, competitions and whatever else they could think of to do with the band. The record label had sent each major station one exclusive track from the album. As a result, Radio 1 played the Crispian Mills track 'Narayan' morning, noon and night, while London's Kiss FM got their hands on 'Mindfields'.

The build-up continued at an incredible rate. The band's numerous Internet sites ran suggestions as to the album's contents, with one running a list of tracks, many of which Liam had never even heard of – titles like the unknown 'Brown' sat next to the well-known tracks like

'Smack My Bitch Up' and 'Funky Shit'. MTV showed The Prodigy's videos constantly, whilst the newspapers ran their own stories by the week, always trying to outdo each other. Chris Sharpe's telephone at XL seemed to be setting alight with the amount of overtime it was doing. Everyone wanted that exclusive, that different angle, that story.

'Actually, everybody wanted to go on the road with the band, to America preferably,' laughs Sharpe. 'I can't even hazard a guess as to how many requests I got daily from papers and magazines saying, "We'll give you the front cover if you give us the US exclusive." It was quite amazing.'

The Fat of the Land had completely taken over Chris's life. But he wasn't alone, as the entire media seemed to have become obsessed with the album as well.

On the last Tuesday of May, exactly one week before the album's release, *Melody Maker* ran an exclusive Prodigy offer entitling readers to receive a specially stamped commemorative copy of the album upon its release. Next to this however was a huge picture of Keith giving a one-fingered salute, whilst a headline read 'GOTCHA! German cops grab Keith Prodigy'. It's the kind of tabloid-baiting press that a press officer would dream of. Flinty getting arrested. Even better was the fact that he had to be dragged off a plane in the process. The spirit of rock'n'roll was alive and well, and living amidst The Prodigy!

Keith saw it simply as a case of pride and prejudice however. In a telephone conversation the following night he explained to me:

'Basically, the guy took a sort of dislike to me from the minute I got on the plane. As soon as I got on he was saying to me, "Are you all right, sir? I think you're hyperactive and not really fit to fly." I was like, 'What the fuck are you on about?" I can't really remember what I was saying at the time because I was so gobsmacked. He was just so patronizing, so the next time he walked past I was like, 'All right?" – you know, all sarcastic like, and he goes, "You're definitely hyperactive, sir." I mean all I was doing was having a laugh with everyone. We were all sitting on the same row so it's not like we were shouting across the cabin. There was raised voices and a little bit of laughter, but that's all.

'I said to one of the female stewardesses, "Oh, what lovely staff we've got." Obviously I was being like one of the lads, but I didn't mean to be offensive to anyone. I mean, if people take offence to me swearing that's their problem. I grew up hearing swearing all the time so it's natural to me and I don't think I should apologize for that.'

MJ: 'Why do you think he singled you out, Keith? I've seen you on planes, you do tend to prefer to stand up and mess around than sit still and behave. Haven't there been times when you've knocked on the cabin doors and asked the pilot if he needed a hand up front? I've even seen you "helping" the stewardesses give the refreshments out.'

Keith: 'Yeah, but that's when we're on private planes. OK, so I've got a sense of humour, but I wasn't doing anything this time. I think he thought I was sort of on drugs or drunk. The way he was trying to talk to me was like a textbook warning. I don't actually think he knew I was in the band. I just think he was the boy at school who got bullied, and now he's getting his own back because, for a short while, he was that bully. I wrote some lyrics about it on the way back, so now I've got a song together.'

MJ: 'Did any of the other passengers complain about you?'

Keith: 'No-one around us seemed to be taking offence to it at all. To be honest when I was getting chucked off the passengers were more pissed off that they were going to be delayed on the runway for an extra half hour while two old bill vans and nine pigs arrived to take me off the plane.'

MJ: 'Wasn't the steward just doing his job?'

Keith: 'No way was he doing his job to the letter of the law. No way at all. I think he was out of order. It was a personal vendetta against the punk. He took out the Air UK no-punk policy and chucked me off. He was reading the small print on the very last page of the rule book. The very small print that reads, "You can be a total areshole to any punk and chuck him off, especially if he uses bad language." It's because he could do it and he wanted to thrive on that minute of power.

'It's never happened to me before. I've been told to calm down a couple of times but that's all. Usually people take me with good humour. I mean, I don't mean offence to anyone. I thrive off incidents like this really. It gave me a buzz but it didn't make me feel so anarchic that I'm about to burn down the local police station. The thing is there's always someone like that around, you just have to be chill about it all. Just another experience.'

MJ: 'So what did the German police do to you?'

Keith: 'The police took me off in their vans and questioned me. Asked me what happened, but there wasn't much of a story to tell 'em. I said to 'em, "You tell people to fuck off, I tell people to fuck off, it's no big deal." It's not as if I was going to nick the plane mid-flight. All they did was run my name through the computer, check I was who I said I was and then asked for my autograph and sent me on my way.'

MJ: 'How did it feel having police with machine guns escorting you?'

Keith: 'To be honest, it didn't bother me that they all had machine guns because that's how you expect them to be over there. I thought the amount of pigs was a bit over the top though. The rest of the lads had a much worse time of it back at Stansted though. When they got back there was loads of them waiting with machine guns and that. Apparently they were saying, "This is our fucking airport, sit down, shut up." It got a bit heated and Leeroy and Maxim had a row with them, just because this one steward had caused so much shit. All because of a bit of bad language and me telling him to fuck off.'

In many ways, this kind of attention had become increasingly a part of Keith's life. With the notoriety of Keith the 'punkin' instigator', people found it increasingly difficult to separate the wild man from the private man. He had seen this firsthand after someone had smashed into his car. While he was sorting the mess out with the other driver, a complete stranger who happened to be walking past approached the crash and offered his thoughts on the subject.

'He starts going, "I know who you are, it's just a fucking car, you can afford it." That annoyed me more than the geezer hitting my car. I mean I wasn't going ballistic and at the same time I wasn't going, "I'm Keith from The Prodigy and you've hit my car." Then this guy's saying, "I thought you believed in karma?" and I'm saying, "Yeah, but not when someone hits my car." Then he called the police and that, but when they arrived they were chill. This guy just wanted to be involved.'

If this wasn't enough, Keith's bad week had been topped off by a stray cat which he'd taken into his house and duly fed and cared for it. As Keith attempted to reassure the frightened moggy it lashed out at him and took a lump out of his finger

'It's horrible, you can still see all of this membrane-type stuff,' he complained. But it wasn't too serious and the cat remained. This run of bad luck would soon be forgotten however, as the album's release date crept ever closer, and anticipation grew.

On Friday 27 June at ten thirty in the morning a small crowd could be seen blocking the doorway to the Our Price Records shop at Waterloo Train Station, London. Closer inspection revealed a shop crammed to the hilt with customers. The reason? They were playing the album in its entirety, on the hour, every hour, for the whole day. The story was the same in all the Our Price shops throughout the country. The fever was building.

Two days later Tower Records in London's Piccadilly Square, along with selected branches of Our Price and Virgin, opened their doors at midnight to sell the album. Fans had queued outside for hours in order to get the first copies which had been stamped with a number and a logo. Amazingly, within those first few hours, 30,000 copies of the album were sold in the UK alone. *The Fat of the Land* looked like turning into one of the fastest sellers ever.

'It's about the third-fastest selling album of all time,' said a confident Chris Sharpe the following day, 'but we're still getting the figures in so that could change.'

Later that day XL Records were able to confirm that *The Fat of the Land* was in fact the number one fastest seller. The album was an unprecedented success. And the band? They were touring. Initially on their all-conquering dates in the States and quickly followed by dates throughout Europe, playing the festival circuit and lapping up all the attention.

*   *   *   *   *

Paris, 15 June 1997.

'Are you the guitar player?' asks the girl whose been sitting by the backstage doors for over an hour.

'No, I'm the keyboard player,' replies Liam, 'do you want to meet the guitarist?'

'No, but I'd die to shag the singer.'

You get this kind of offer when you're in The Prodigy.

The whole band are suffering from the fatigue of an impossible tour schedule. In an attempt to overcome the numbing tiredness, Keith opts to use the services of the promoter's acupuncturist girlfriend.

'That cheered me up no end,' he exclaims, while inspecting his skin for pinpricks, his eyes beaming with the enthusiasm of someone who has just discovered a new buzz. This is what it's all about for Keith. Living on the energy of it all. Fulfilling a never-ending quest for 'the experience'. The rest of The Prodigy mill round the dressing room. Maxim sits in stony silence. He has barely said a word since we left the hotel, as if he's vibing himself up. This is Maxim's way, quietly observing, taking it all in until, after what seems like hours, or even days of silence, he comes out with a comment which astounds everyone, or a wisecrack which floors the band with laughter. His humour is as dry as a desert wind and as sharp as a needle. It's matched only by his love of a bit of mischief.

Where Maxim appears to be the silent observer, involved yet somehow distant, Liam's quietness seems generated by the need to keep control of things. He wears the responsibility on his face, lines are prematurely beginning to etch themselves into his skin, as if the stress has left a permanent mark for him to contemplate. Lounging in the plastic garden chairs which the promoters have provided in the name of comfort, Liam stares at the ground, occasionally looking up to greet one of the others. Every now and then he stands up and wanders around the room, mentally preparing himself for the show. Paris isn't one of their favourite places to play – the crowd aren't really up for it – and there's undoubtedly potential for a huge amount of tension in the air.

However The Prodigy come with their own in-built stress-relief team – Keith, Leeroy and guitarist Gizz Butt. Leeroy leans over the small table, skinning up a huge spliff – the latest in a long line. Occasionally he looks up, with a grin that says it all. Here he is, about to go on stage to do his favourite thing, dance, he's surrounded by his mates and he's got a seemingly endless supply of dope. What could provide better job satisfaction than that?

'I'm really into that *Formula 1* game at the moment.' We're talking Playstation again, it's a common bond. 'I've got two machines set up at home with two TVs, so I can race my mates. Actually it helps me calm down, you know what I mean. I already smoke too much spliff so that doesn't calm me any more, so I have a go on the Playstation instead.'

'He's an addict all right,' adds one of his friends.

'I tell you what, I don't care if he's addicted to friggin' petrol fumes, just so long as he hurries up with that spliff,' interjects Gizz, laughing.

Gizz is the perfect foil for the rest of the band. Where Leeroy is a practical joker, Gizz is a stand-up comedian. His continuous stream of jokes may be as old as the leather jacket he wears, but they sound incredibly funny coming from his lips. He's a natural. He makes the others laugh, which is important. And apart from that, he's the fuel in the fire of Liam's machinery. Gizz plays hard, Liam pushes it harder. Gizz turns it up to eleven, Liam goes through the sound barrier. Gizz has become an integral part of The Prodigy live show.

The final and most visual cog in the wheel is Keith. He's smaller in the flesh, but somehow bigger as well. He's like a bulldog, small but packing more bite than a lion. As he paces the room cracking jokes, mind working overtime, it's hard to believe that he doesn't take fast drugs at gigs any more. He's naturally wired, excited by the very energy of being there, in the best band in the world. The Prodigy would be the band he would want to be in if he wasn't already there, smack bang in the middle of it all. Being in The Prodigy has allowed Keith to exercise two very different facets of his personality.

Two nights previously, on Friday 13th, Keith's more dangerous personality could be seen in brighter colours than ever before. Already noted for his on-stage antics, Keith's natural anger toppled over the edge in front of a packed crowd in Germany. Everything that could go wrong, did. The sound was bad, the equipment kept breaking down and the band just wanted to be elsewhere. Suddenly the sound cut out, like a pre-Glastonbury warning. Keith just flipped.

'It was full-on aggression. On a kind of basic anger level, I really enjoyed it. Everything was fucking up and there was this geezer filming. I was like, "Now this is pissing me off, there's someone in the audience filming us," so I ran over there, grabbed the camera, took it to the back of the stage and smashed it into pieces.'

Liam: 'Yeah, afterwards Keith was like, "Somebody was filming but I got rid of the camera," and John [the tour manager] was just going, "No way, man, they were meant to be there, they were from some cable TV company."'

Keith: 'Ha! The look on their fucking face when I got the camera . . . they were shitting themselves.'

Liam: 'It was violent but it was punk rock!'

It was also a blinding performance. The anger on stage fired up the crowd like nothing else. You could taste the energy, as Keith often puts it.

Paris was dull in comparison. The audience were flat, the night rain cooled down the vibe considerably, and the band responded.

'I hate it when things don't go right. It just pisses me off,' confides Maxim later. 'I take it quite personally, I just think I could have done a lot better myself. Somehow I let the others down.'

After the show, the dressing room turns into a full-on industry bash. Members of Rage Against the Machine talk to the band, a young Vanessa

Paradis look-a-like hunts down autographs, while outside The Prodigy tribute band – called, naturally enough, The Jilted Generation – try every trick in the book to get to meet their idols.

As soon as Liam realizes that they're there, he walks outside. It's typical of him and, indeed, the rest of the band. They still refuse to act like stars. And besides, The Jilted Generation have come over here at their own expense, without a hotel or any form of accommodation sorted out. Liam has to respect his fans, especially when they're willing to go to such massive extremes.

Back at the hotel, the band decide to head straight to their rooms. It's not been the best night in their lives, but there's always tomorrow to look forward to.

As Leeroy walks into the lift he turns round and holds open the elevator doors with both arms outstretched. His face contorts with the strain, as if he's trying to stop the walls themselves from caving in. Before finally letting go he cracks one more joke: 'I was going to be a Gladiator but they wanted to call me Rancho and I couldn't get along with the cowboy boots they wanted me to wear.'

The whole entourage burst into laughter. It hasn't been such a bad night after all.

*　*　*　*　*

In the middle of all this, however, came a sizable dampener on the band's spirits. The first review appeared in a national publication and it slammed the album. Running with the review a week earlier than anyone else, *Melody Maker*'s David Stubbs condemned the band for the album's relative lack of surprises and declaring it to be, 'the music of MTV's dreams. Rock'n'roll tamed by capitalism, as much to do with "radicalism" as Billy Idol, snowboarding or Hooch. It's the perfect soundtrack to the delinquent, hedonistic consumerism of these times, with no idea other than to just forge ahead, bigger and badder than the rest.'

Stubbs also objected to the delays on the album, suggesting that they'd merely been a cynical marketing device on Liam's part.

In an article in the trade magazine *Music Week* a couple of days later, XL's Richard Russell was quoted as saying, 'The wait has definitely worked in our favour. It would have been different if the band had been out of the public eye, like the Stereo MCs for example. But they have been putting out singles and increasing awareness of their music all over the world. Now everyone is desperate to get their hands on this album.'

In defence of Liam's lateness with the album, in the same article, Mike Champion goes on to say, 'you only have to listen to the songs to understand why this album could never have appeared overnight. It is a ground breaker in terms not only of the sound, but also the effort, time and skill that has gone into it. Every single track is on a different tip. It's an album that will stand on its own for a very long time to come.'

The Fat of the Land was every inch a Prodigy album – exactly what any loyal fan would have expected of them. It contained the recent singles 'Firestarter' and 'Breathe', as well as a number of tracks which the band had been playing live through the last eighteen months: 'Funky Shit', 'Mindfields', 'Smack My Bitch Up' (with its loop lifted from the Beastie Boys' 'Root Down') and the L7 cover 'Fuel My Fire'. In effect, only four of the tracks were new to the fans. But then this album was intended to be a snapshot of the band's live show.

'The thing is, I absolutely hate live albums, so this was supposed to be like a representation of our live show,' explains Liam. 'But there's stuff in there that goes a lot further. Tracks we'll never play live. But that review really pissed us off. I mean he didn't even get all of his facts right.'

'To be honest, I wasn't surprised, because that's what papers do, isn't it?' sighs Keith. 'See us get successful and then knock us down. But I was angry for Liam's sake. I mean, he'd fucking worked himself stupid to make this album. I'd go round to his gaff and he'd be like stressed to fuck because he had to finish the thing by a deadline. People don't see that. And then this geezer comes along and just dissed thousands of hours of hard work. It's just sick really. That's why I don't read the press any more.'

Perhaps one of the most upsetting things about this bad review was the fact that up until now *Melody Maker* had always been behind The Prodigy. They gave them their first national interview. The band's favourite article, written by Simon Price, had been a *Melody Maker* cover story the previous summer. And now this.

However, it would seem that David Stubbs was quite alone in his negativity about the album. Everyone else loved it.

So what was all the fuss about? Ten tracks of breakbeat techno with a punk attitude. Ten of the fiercest cuts to have entered the pop lexicon. A full-on roller-coaster of an album which seemed way too short – even after the first listen it left you wanting much more.

Amongst the new tracks were the much talked about collaborations. 'Diesel Power' saw Kool Keith, originally of The Ultramagnetc MCs and latterly known as Dr Octagon, providing some wild and surreal rhymes. Meanwhile 'Narayan', featuring Crispian Mills of UK indie rock band Kula Shaker, was a collaboration which brought with it a whole heap of controversy. Crispian Mills had recently been quoted in a magazine as having sympathies with certain aspects of Nazi ideology. Furthermore, it turned out that when he was younger a previous band of his had played at a conference for Britain's extreme right wing. 'Crispian the Nazi' was the news story of the time. Liam wasn't concerned, however.

'I don't think that "Crispian is a Nazi" rubbish will affect us because it's the tune he's done that matters. I mean, he could have shot someone and I wouldn't care. At the end of the day it's a good tune. It doesn't mean anything to me. I don't know the full story anyway, and I don't want to know. I worked with Crispian because I like the sound of his voice. It was nothing to do with him as a person.'

'Narayan' represented Liam at his most commercial. An Eastern refrain unfolds into a hard groove with Mill's sugar-sweet vocal singing over the top about the Western Sun, until it all builds toward a climactic ending with Mills providing one of his famed mantras. Says Liam, 'When we were recording that track it wasn't supposed to be like a "Prodigy meets Kula Shaker" type of thing. I wanted the sound of Crispian's voice on the track. When he mentioned a mantra I was like, "Hold up, I don't know about that." I just didn't want it to have that Indian Kula Shaker vibe but when I put the mantra onto the track I just thought "fucking hell, it really works". I reckon a lot of people are going to go into that track thinking they're not going to like it and then come out the other side loving it. When I'd finished the track Crispian tried to do an edited Kula Shaker version, to try and make it like his own track, which is cool, but it didn't really work. It's not a pop song, it needs to be a long track that builds.'

In retrospect, it turned out to be one of the album's strongest numbers. The controversy failed to go away, but Liam and the others had come to disregard this kind of negative attention. Ever since the so-called 'arsonists' anthem', 'Firestarter', first became a shock story in the tabloid press, The Prodigy had come to expect it.

However 'Smack My Bitch Up', the album's opener, had apparently got the band's American label up in arms. One of the biggest US chain stores had refused to stock the album if it bore that title. It was a controversial B-boy-inspired track which lifted a sample from 'Give the Drummer Some' by the Ultramagnetic MCs and it immediately elicited attacks from the self-appointed moral guardians of the world.

'It's a B-boy thing,' claims Liam. 'I'm not saying, "Go out and beat up your girlfriends and wives." A bitch doesn't have to mean a woman. There are so many other connotations.'

The chain store wasn't convinced. Indeed, they had also complained about 'Funky Shit', so in the end the band were forced to change the titles for the US market to 'Smack My B**** Up' and 'Funky S***'. Amazingly, the country which boasts one of the highest crime rates in the world, where a gun is fired every second of the day, found it hard to accept the words 'Bitch' and 'Shit'.

'One of the reasons I signed to Maverick was because they promised us complete artistic control, and now this happens. I just don't know what to think,' complains Liam. 'But if not changing the title means that the album's only going to be available in a few shops in the country, then I can't really argue.'

The final version of the album also omitted two of the rumoured collaborative songs. Firstly the track that Liam had recorded with Skin from Skunk Anansie had, he said, been dropped because the combination of his music and her voice ended up as too poppy.

'I really like her voice, you know, but what she did on my track just didn't work well enough to be released. It was just too commercial, kind of a sell-out song. Actually, I never even said that it was going to be on the album although she'd told everyone, so I didn't exactly drop it. I didn't know what the final track listing was going to be until it was finished, so that Skin track was never a definite.'

The second track that failed to materialize was perhaps a little more disappointing. Liam had been working on a track which started quietly and just grew to massive proportions, filled to the brim with rushing breaks and powerhouse techno flourishes. The guest vocalist he had in mind was Perry Farrell, previously with the legendary Jane's Addiction, now with Porno for Pyros. It was a coming together which seemed inspired. Farrell's bittersweet, snaking vocal lines melting into Liam's epic electronic funk would surely be the highlight of the album. But in the event the meeting never actually happened.

'Perry Farrell is out there, I'm telling you now, he's out there,' laughs Liam with astonishment. 'Trying to have a conversation with him was hopeless. We were sitting there, you know, telling him how we were into his stuff and how we'd love to do his Lollapalooza some time. And he starts saying, "I don't do that any more, man. Now we have a new thing, it's in the sky and the people are angels and this is how we're gonna get them there." Totally fucking off it. Next thing I know, he calls me at home and asks if we can do his new tour that he was setting up. And I said yeah. Then we got to talking and the idea of him guesting comes up. He was totally into it. He was absolutely together on the phone, which was what I couldn't understand. He started going on on about these vibes, and he seemed like he was on the ball. After the conversation I was like really excited about it all so I started on this track. Then the dates for his tour thing came through and I looked at my schedule but we already had a lot of festivals booked up and we basically couldn't make it. So we phoned him back and said unfortunately we can't make the gig. And he said, "If you can't do the gig, I can't do the track." That track was written with him in mind and I can't picture anyone else with it. I had to get rid of it. I thought the whole thing was a bit shitty really.'

*   *   *   *   *

Despite these minor hiccups, within a week of release the album had gone to number one in twenty-two countries around the world. The only territory which didn't give up the top slot was France where they crashed in at number two. A week later *The Fat of the Land* took over the number one position. In the UK its sales in the first week were in excess of all of the sales of the rest of the top fifty put together. Indeed, it was outselling the number two album *OK Computer* by the hugely popular indie band, Radiohead, by eight copies to one.

When Liam found out about the situation he spent hours phoning everyone he could think of. It was a record situation, and one which surprised even the most informed industry pundits. According to the Soundscan figures in the US, *The Fat of the Land* scored an amazing 200,959 sales in its first week alone. By comparison, the number two album at the time, the original soundtrack to the Hollywood box-office smash, *Men in Black*, only achieved sales of 177,470. Interestingly, the band which occupied third place was UK's biggest band The Spice Girls whose album *Spice* had managed a meagre 147,922 sales. Clearly *The Fat of the Land* was outstripping everyone by a huge margin.

'It's pretty unreal, to be honest,' exclaimed a shocked Liam to the *NME*. 'It'll fuck a lot of people off in America and that's what we like. There are some fucking fifty-year-old journalists who've disrespected us. Some of the traditionalists, who are stuck in their normal rock'n'roll methods, and they don't see any angle on it.

'It just shows you don't have to go over there and do bullshit interviews, the music speaks for itself,' he continued. 'We've got to number one by doing it ourselves. I rang Keith and he was pretty stoned. He went silent for thirty seconds and then kept saying, "Fuck, fuck, fuck."'

Ironically, at the same time as this astounding achievement, Oasis had been quoted in the press as having said that they were bigger than God, obviously a reference to The Beatles' well-known quote about being more famous than Jesus. However, many of the papers posed the question, 'If Oasis are bigger than God, how big are The Prodigy then?' It's a question which Liam just shrugs off. He has said that he considers Oasis and The Spice Girls to be famous, not The Prodigy.

'Believe me, when the Oasis album comes out it'll wipe us clean off the board,' continued Liam in the same *NME* interview. 'Everyone would just expect us to go back there [America] and hammer it, just play and play and play. I know that's what the record company are going to be thinking but we're not going to do that. I'm not fucking killing myself for nobody.

'I think the record company are going to be really surprised at our reaction, because we're not going to go running around screaming "we're number one". We're not going out to try and crack it. That's a bit of a business thing. All we ever wanted to do was go over there and play music to the people.'

Incredibly humble sentiments which had a lot of people cynically retorting that Liam himself must be a businessman to have worked out this particular marketing strategy. It would, in fact, be fair to say that this attitude of only ever playing things their own way was one of the biggest contributing factors to the band's success. Success in America, although fantastic news, wasn't the be-all and end-all to The Prodigy. And Liam had seen enough bands swallowed whole by the US in an attempt to remain in the American public's consciousness. The Prodigy, on the other hand, fully intended to keep it under control, feet firmly on the ground, keeping it real.

Amidst the excitement about the album sales came another

controversy. This time it wasn't aimed at the band but at the selling practices of some of the shops. British chain store Asda had been caught selling the album two days before its release, in order to capitalize on the album's demand. The only way they could do this was by avoiding putting the sales through the computer system via which the charts are complied, and, as a result, the album wasn't credited for a huge amount of sales.

Nevertheless, two months later the album was still sitting at the top of the pile throughout the world. It was a record that Oasis were unable to beat with the release of their third album *Be Here Now*, despite industry predictions. Sure, it out-sold *The Fat of the Land* in the UK, but on a worldwide scale, it didn't come close.

The Prodigy were now one of the biggest bands in the world!

*   *   *   *   *

At a time when The Prodigy should have been celebrated in the press for their achievements, they were, instead, once again in the middle of controversy. The sleeve artwork for *The Fat of the Land* featured a quote running through its booklet which had been appropriated from a speech made by Nazi Luftwaffe commander Hermann Goering, which read: 'We have no butter, but I ask you, would you rather have butter or guns? Shall we import lard or steel? Let me tell you, preparedness makes us powerful. Butter merely makes us fat.' The inside cover of the booklet merely contained the words 'Steel' and 'Lard' respectively. Liam had read the quote in a book which which he'd been given one Christmas and it had struck him how powerful the words were. It seemed to him to be the first B-boy quote. When the discussions came for the cover artwork he knew exactly what he wanted it to say.

But he hadn't counted on the reaction it would receive. In a typically dismissive act he just shrugged off the critics who 'were just looking for shit to throw at us. If they think that we're Nazi sympathizers then they're stupid. I mean we've got black dudes in the band, we're not Nazis.'

'That quote is supposed to be like a sample, you know,' he continues. 'That's how I write my music – take things from one place and put them into another, to create a new meaning. That's what I did with that quote. Lifted out of context it has nothing to do with Nazis or whatever – it's something completely different.'

However it was a furore which continued to dog the band for the next few months, with every journalist asking the same Nazi-sympathy questions: why that quote, and why work with Crispian Mills? Liam's answer was always a variation on the same theme. He had no regrets, he meant nothing political and yes, he was very happy with the end results, thank you very much.

Perhaps a more accurate reason for the album's title and that lard-obsessed quote was closer to real life than people thought. Both Liam and Keith were increasingly aware of their own excess fat. Not that they were in any way large, but when you're on stage with two of the fittest and leanest people in the music world (Maxim and Leeroy), a few extra pounds around the midriff is sure to affect you a bit.

*   *   *   *   *

'Ladies and gentlemen, I give you the best Prodigy tribute band in the world, The Australian Prodigy!'

The comedian and compère, and good friend of the band, Dennis Pennis runs off stage as the opening chords to '2001: A Space Odyssey' roar out of the huge speakers. From the stage, the view offers one of the most depressing sights ever. An endless sea of mud and drenched bodies, shivering in the coldest and wettest June on record. But this is supposed to be the festival which celebrates the summer solstice. Glastonbury, the biggest and best music festival there is.

Keith runs on stage, sidestepping the puddles and clumps of mud which have been slung onto the stage.

'Fucking hell. FUCKING HELL!' he shouts in complete astonishment at what he's seeing. 'Smack My Bitch Up' erupts across the immense field as the pyramid stage springs to life for one of the most eagerly awaited performances of the night. The Prodigy's last Glastonbury gig was the stuff of legends, the night that saw them totally lose their rave baggage. The press reports on the band's current tour read like a list of superlatives, and Glastonbury? It's the last gig before the album finally comes out. It is, as some people suggest, the band's most important gig to date.

But the weather isn't bothered about careers and as Liam leans over his hardware, manipulating the band's fourth song 'Breathe', it all goes very wrong. Rain gets into the machines and the whole thing grinds to a halt. A deafening silence spreads across Glastonbury, as Maxim storms off stage. They've no idea what's going on.

The crowd grow restless. They've stood in mud all day exposed to the cold, got flu, trench foot and a thousand other ailments which walk hand in hand with such abhorrent conditions, and the very band they've come to see would appear to have cut their set short! Mud gets slung and abuse is hurled and the only person who will go near the stage is Dennis Pennis. He's a brave man – or stupid. Or both. He calms the crowd down, tells a few jokes which some people even laugh at. Huge numbers just walk away, looking for another set by another band in one of the adjacent fields.

Twenty minutes later The Prodigy return. They play four more songs before ending with the crowd-pleaser 'Firestarter'. It's a disaster.

'Oh well,' says Liam philosophically, afterwards, 'we can't be blamed for the rain. But it wasn't too bad really. When we came back it really kicked off, and anyway by the time we'd played "Breathe" I knew that we had the audience. We were rocking.'

Nevertheless, the band aren't at all happy.

* * * * *

What's the single most irritating habit of anyone else in the band?
Maxim: 'Keith. Lateness, pondering around. "Oh, I'll just do this, I'll just do that." It just winds me up. And it's been going on for about five years.'
Leeroy: 'Keith. Without a doubt. He's got loads of 'em. Never go shopping with Keith – worse than any bird you could imagine.'
Liam: 'Keith. His arse goes off like an alarm bell at six o'clock every morning.'
Keith: 'Erm. Nothing, really. No-one really annoys me.'
Adam Higginbotham, Select

Liam's house, Braintree, 3 July 1997.

'Can't get to the phone right now, so leave a message after the tone.'

The phone rings constantly. As soon as one message is completed another one comes through. It's completely insane, but Liam seems to be used to this kind of thing. After all, he is one of the most in-demand artists of the moment.

'Yeah Liam, mate, well done, nice one. Talk later mate.' Click, buzz.

'Liam, it's Chris [XL PR] here, I've got Melody Maker hassling me for a quote about the sleeve notes.' Click, buzz.

'Liam, there's some shit going down about that band Jedi Knights. They reckon you've not cleared a sample of one of their tracks. Call me.' Click, buzz.

'Liam, good news, man. The album's mid-week chart position in America is number one! It's fucking brilliant.' Click, buzz.

Each time the phone rings the caller seems to bring a different set of fortunes. On the one hand the album's success, on the other – well there's that controversy thing that won't go away.

'I tell you what, people just want to make a story out of anything. But I'm not bothered really, the papers have got to sell copies and if it's me that's going to help that, what can I do?' says Liam.

His house is set at the end of a gravel drive. From the outside it's just a small coachhouse-style affair with a Volkswagen camper van, complete with smoked windows, parked alongside an AC Cobra 427. Going inside, however, isn't unlike walking into Dr Who's Tardis. The large hallway is decorated in a mock Aztec style. It's like a set from *Indiana Jones*, or even the computer game 'Tomb Raider', which had the entire band hooked when it came out.

To the right of the hall lies 'Earthbound', Liam's studio, which has not only seen most of The Prodigy's material come to life, but also untold potential masterpieces consigned to the scrapheap because they didn't meet with Liam's exacting demands.

To the left lies the living room. On one side stands a huge broadsword, on the other a massive coffin, complete with giant bolts, which opens to reveal a drinks cabinet. The rest of the room is dominated by an original Dalek from the *Dr Who* TV series. The room is surprisingly free of Prodigy-related paraphernalia. Only the original artwork for the inside cover of *Music for the Jilted Generation* provides any hint as to the owner's identity. That and the two MTV awards chucked in the corner.

'I'm moving soon,' declares Liam as he pours out some coffee. 'All of the people in Braintree, well they've known me since I was a kid and now that I'm, like, well known as The Prodigy, they all know where I live. So when someone comes to town looking for me they just tell them.'

Liam's house has become an easy target for fans keen to meet their hero. But such attention is no stranger to him. As far back as 1992, when Liam was still living with his father some fans came over from Germany to hunt down the man behind their favourite band. At this time the chemically induced *bonhomie* that surrounded the rave scene forged many a strong and lasting friendship. Unfortunately, it also brought with it unwanted new friends who would mistake the E smile as a sign of friendship beyond the call of duty. In those days it wasn't unusual for Liam, Leeroy, Keith and Maxim to go out into the crowd after a PA and dance with them. After all, they were party people themselves. Unfortunately, a couple of Prodigy fans in Germany mistook this for an open invitation to invade the band's lives.

One night, Liam came home with his girlfriend to find these German girls he could hardly remember sitting in the living room. Apparently they'd arrived earlier that day, asked some local kids where they could find The Prodigy, and had then followed directions to Liam's dad's place. They proceeded to inform Mr Howlett senior that they were good mates of his son and could they wait for him? When Liam came home he was, to say the least, unhappy with the situation.

Such invasions of privacy became an increasingly regular occurrence for the whole band. There have been times when fans would literally camp out at the end of Liam's drive, or Keith's front door, hanging around for hours for little more than a quick chat. Or even just a 'Hello'. For the lads who had long fought hard against being perceived as stars, the whole situation was a bit strange. But nothing was as weird as the time, soon after 'Firestarter' came out, that Liam's own place came under siege from an irate member of the public.

'I've had some right fucking nonces turn up on my doorstep,' exclaims Liam. 'I actually had a fight with this one geezer at one o'clock in the morning. This guy was at my door and he confronted me. He was a religious freak who thought we had a thing about hell. I was just stunned, you know what I mean. But he wouldn't let it go, he just kept on about me being some kind of devil worshipper or something. In the end he tried to push his way into my house. So I just pushed him back. It was fucking annoying, I can tell you. But people seem to think it's OK to invade my life. Like with the Internet. I hate the Internet, it's a piece of shit. It's just a web of useless information. You can't stop what people do on it. I mean, I turned on the other day, looking at this Prodigy site and my house was on the Internet. My fucking house! It was like, "Let's look around Liam's house." You click on it and there's all these picture of my house taken from different angles. Then it was, "Let's look at Liam's studio," and I was like, "Fuck me, they must have broken in or something." Luckily it was only photos from an old magazine feature I did, but the thought of people hanging around my house and taking pictures for the Internet just fucks me right off. It's too weird.'

For Keith, things have got to the point where he can't walk through the streets of his hometown of Braintree for fear of hassle. So instead he rides his motorbike everywhere. People know who it is when he speeds past them, but they don't get the chance to bother him. He is also having a house built in the Essex countryside. It will be next door to Liam's.

'People have got the idea that I'm going to be living in this mansion and Keith's going to be living in the gatehouse, like I'm lord of the manor or something. Actually it's more like the other way round because he's got more land than me.'

Sitting on the huge sofa, Liam seems like a clock which has been almost overwound. The hard work over the last few years, the blinding intensity of finishing that album and the unbelievable strain of the recent American trip where they had their first real taste of the power of the American media circus, have all left him exhausted. Yet he's still buzzing like a man whose mission is hardly complete. Sure, the album seems to be doing OK, well, more than OK, incredibly well, but there's so much more he wants to achieve.

The band have got five days off in their current schedule. It's Liam's first break since 'Firestarter' was released. Leeroy and Maxim are at home chilling with their girlfriends, Keith is busy working on the new house. And Liam? He's decided to record a track with Tom Morello from Rage Against the Machine. It's for a soundtrack to the film *Spawn*, and for the first time a song will be credited as a Prodigy collaboration. The Prodigy versus Tom Morello connection came about following a request from the Rage guitarist who put down some of his trademark funky riffs and a few wild guitars on DAT tape and sent them to Liam to manipulate.

'I'm really enjoying doing it. You know, the only pressure is time but I don't have to worry about it being seen as a Prodigy song, I can experiment a bit more. Actually, I'm thinking of maybe doing another track with the stuff Tom's sent. I'd quite like to work like this more in the future, because I really like to work on my own. This way I get some creative input from people I really respect, and then give it that Prodigy twist at the end. It's a cool way of working.'

On that early July day, sitting in a pair of old board shorts, playing constantly with his sunglasses, Liam is hardly able to contain his excitement at the continued barrage of telephone calls which have punctuated the whole day. At the message about underground electro outfit Jedi Nights chasing him about his use of a break from one of their tracks on 'Climbatize', Liam looks bemused. 'But they've just lifted it from a breaks album themselves. I don't know, I really love their stuff but you know, there's like a code about sampling. If the break's yours, then yeah, you've got a point. If it's not originally yours and you want payment on it then . . . well, it's not on, is it?'

As the message comes through about the album being confirmed in its mid-week number-one position in America, his grin would put Charly the Cheshire Cat to shame, but he's still calm. However when Leeroy's voice comes over the answer phone, excitedly talking about a picture of Keith in that day's issue of the *Sun*, Liam bursts out laughing and runs to the phone.

'Liam, man, pick up the phone, you've got to see this picture of Keith done up as Leo Sayer, it's fucking hilarious, man.' Amidst the chaos of the recent times, and standing on the verge of world-wide success big-style, Liam's laughter gives it all away. He is still that bloke from Braintree who likes to hang out with his mates and to party.

In the living room, the crunch of tyres breaking on gravel can be heard. The doorbell rings and in walks Keith Flint. His hair has been dyed black in a direct response to the unbelievable amount of attention (recently extremely unwanted) his multi-coloured look has had. He looks harder, a bit more punky, but his smile speaks volumes. In his hand he clutches a copy of the *Sun*. He strides into the room and another look crosses his face. A momentary look of shock as he sees me. He instantly sees a reporter, a journalist, and for a second, a look of a someone being caught off guard, in a private moment, flashes across his face.

He looks over at Liam and his expression returns to the broad smile. The sight of Keith in Leo Sayer Afro wig is too much. The pair just laugh aloud. Like a couple of mates on an adventure. Only this one is just about to go into orbit.

* * * * *

The Jedi Knights fiasco refused to die quickly. The band claimed that Liam had directly lifted a rhythm loop from one of their tracks called 'Drums from Outer Bongolia' and used it on his own 'Climbatize'. Liam instantly retorted with the claim that they'd lifted it in the first place. In fact the original break could be found on an obscure album by an act called The Incredible Bongo Band. It had been their cover version of Cliff Richard and the Shadows' hit 'Apache' which gave way to the seminal 'Apache' break which became a mainstay in the world of hip hop and drum'n'bass.

The track used by both The Jedi Knights and Liam Howlett was called 'Bongolia Beat', a fact that Liam was quick to recognize. In a strange twist, Liam did actually admit to having sampled the break from The Jedi Knights, but he refused to pay for it since they'd lifted it in the first place. Realizing that they were pretty angry about the situation, Liam went on to offer the band a Prodigy remix, something which would guarantee huge sales and probably make the band a lot more money than they'd get in the courts. But they declined.

In retrospect, The Jedi Knights, aka Global Communications, were stupid to have gone in so hard about the lift. Their music is littered with samples and it's a safe bet that they'd assumed that Liam wouldn't know his stuff. So when they argued that they'd worked hard on the sample, re-programming it and cutting it up to turn it into their own work, Liam was instantly able to see that this wasn't actually the case. However, his break appeared exactly the same as the original on The Jedi Knights track.

This situation was perhaps indicative of the dance underground's view of Liam. It was easy to assume that since he'd been having hit singles since he was a teenager, and because of his often verbalized dislike of the contemporary club scene, he'd not be as educated in beat science as the underground. In reality, Liam had been immersed in breakbeat culture for fifteen years and could trainspot breakbeats with the best of them. And his ear had continued to be open to the fresh sounds coming through.

It was a particularly strange time for The Jedi Knights as it was. They'd just offered a remix to a Depeche Mode single, which had done exceptionally well in the States. Until now The Jedi Knights had been able to operate without any hassle in the localized surroundings of the UK dance underground. But as soon as their music reached an international audience, the inevitable happened. George Lucas, the inventor of *Star Wars*, noticed that there was a band using one of his trademarked names. He immediately filed a lawsuit against the label (*Mute* in America) and the band.

As for The Prodigy situation? It remained unsolved, although rumours were circulating that Martin Mills, MD of Beggars Banquet who publish Liam, had been to America, and discovered that no-one actually owned the publishing rights to 'Bongolia Beat'. With an open chequebook in hand he tracked down the members of The Incredible Bongo Band, and allegedly bought the rights on the spot. After years of being sampled, the originals had finally seen some money for themselves and, if the rumour is true, The Prodigy's parent label now owned the sample, which in turn meant that The Jedi Knights owed *them*, and not the other way round.

But this is all business stuff, things which Liam and the band claim to try to avoid. It's why they have managers. Nevertheless, it's hard to imagine Liam Howlett letting anyone so much as break wind on behalf of the band until he'd first given it his seal of approval.

SIX

Give Me Some of That Funky Shit

The Prodigy thing is still all about that new experience. We try to keep things fresh by not rehearsing, we try to blend little self-contained tours into the festivals.

Keith, May 1997

V97 Festival, Leeds, 17 August.

Almost two months since the ill-fated Glastonbury gig, The Prodigy return to their home soil for the Virgin-backed festival. Wandering through the guest enclosure, Gizz walks up to me, grabs me from behind and holds me in a headlock.

'All right, geezer?' Gizz is on top form, smile beaming from ear to ear. His spiked hair has been bleached, with blue tips added.

'What you done to your hair, Gizz? It's like blue rinse, man. You're trying to be like that old woman from *Coronation Street*, aren't you?'

'Piss off!' he laughs. 'I'm off to see The Foo Fighters. You coming?'

'Nah mate, I'm going back to see the others.'

Backstage, Liam and Keith are chilling in one of the three Portacabins that act as the band's dressing rooms. They're about as relaxed as I've ever seen them. Certainly Liam appears to be a changed man from the one I saw in Europe only a few weeks earlier. The stress lines have gone, his skin has taken on a healthy glow and his eyes are shining. He looks happy.

'I've just been a lot better since the album came out,' he explains. 'I've got no pressures now. All I have to do is sit back and enjoy it all.'

We quickly decide to follow Gizz to the main stage to see The Foo Fighters. They're Dave Grohl's new band and a bit of a mutual appreciation society has emerged between them and The Prodigy. On the way to the Foos we decide to take a look at the British trip hop outfit, The Sneaker Pimps, in the dance enclosure. The Pimps have only recently put out a cover version of 'Firestarter', but Liam's not really into it.

'Crap, isn't it?' denounces Liam, as Keith raises his eyes to the sky in a look of absolute disdain, before Liam continues, 'That Liam geezer from The Sneaker Pimps phoned me up at about three in the morning going, "I heard you didn't like our version and I was just checking there wasn't any bad blood between us. We only did it out of respect." I was like, "I don't like it, no, but so what?" I mean, I like The Sneaker Pimps but I don't really understand why they've done "Firestarter".'

As we take up our positions to the side of the stage, it becomes clear just how popular The Prodigy have become. Members of the audience catch a glimpse of Keith and Liam, and within seconds the whole of the crowd seem to be ignoring the band who are playing, concentrating instead on the band who are going to be headlining tonight. Suddenly, sections of the audience start cheering, as if Keith is about to run on stage and guest during a version of 'Firestarter'. Hardly likely, considering the duo's feelings about the Pimps' version. As more of the crowd start to cheer, Liam and Keith turn and leave.

The same thing happens on the main stage, as everyone who spots the members of The Prodigy start calling out. For the band who used to go raving with the crowd straight after they'd finished a PA, this celebrity status is a strange aspect of their success. They realize that they can't easily walk out among the crowd any more. If they did they'd get swamped. Just one look at the hundreds of Keith look-a-likes in their Prodigy T-shirts and multi-coloured hair is enough to underline just how much the fans love The Prodigy. And the chance to say hello, get a photo taken with them or perhaps even get an autograph would, for thousands of people here today, be a dream come true.

This becomes all too clear as we wander back through the guest enclosure and Keith and Liam are mobbed by autograph hunters, journalists, photographers and student radio stations begging the boys to record quick interviews. They oblige happily, not in the least fazed by the scene.

'A lot of these people are mates back here,' stresses Liam. 'If not, they're like the little brothers and sisters of our mates, you know what I mean. So it would be hypocritical if I didn't have time for them.'

'We still don't see ourselves as stars, you see,' adds Keith, 'we're just us. The only people who go on about how big we are is the press.' The Prodigy, it would seem, are famous in everyone else's minds but their own.

Liam doesn't look altogether happy with the amount of attention he receives, however. 'I didn't think people would recognize me with my new haircut.' He's joking, of course. He's only had a couple of inches cut off.

The two are soon joined by Leeroy, who stands and chats, signing photos, programmes, T-shirts and anything else that comes to hand. Suddenly Maxim speeds past in a golfing buggy. The backstage area is so far from the main stage that these buggys have been provided to help transport things quickly. Maxim thinks they've been put there for the band's enjoyment. Keith jumps on board and the two of them speed off, weaving in and out of stunned people, heading straight for the arena itself.

An hour later, we're sitting outside the band's dressing rooms with a small group of people, when suddenly Maxim's mean machine spins around the corner. With his foot pressed hard on the throttle, the buggy is aimed directly at us. Maxim's eyes are filled with villainous mischief, whilst his silver-capped teeth glint in the late-afternoon sun. Keith has a look of total pleasure, egging on his partner. At the last moment, Maxim swerves and takes out a load of plastic garden chairs and a table. The pair are in fits of laughter. Everyone else quickly follows suit.

'Morning,' says Keith with a deadpan seriousness that comedian Max Wall would have been proud of.

'Fucking hell, man, we went out into the main arena,' screams Maxim, barely able to control his excitement. 'It was insane. There was this band playing over the other side of the site and we just ran over their drum kit. People were cheering us on!'

This is why people love the idea of The Prodigy. They're a gang, a bunch of lads having a crack – living for the experience.

* * * * *

I saw them last year when they supported Oasis and I hadn't really known much about them then. But they were completely mind blowing. Better than the main band I reckon. I've never seen a band like them. They're so full of energy, it's like electricity. And the music . . . well, let's just say if Oasis had half of their power they wouldn't

**need to do the amount of drugs they do. Apart from that though Maxim
is the horniest singer on the planet.**

Simone Hall, Newcastle. Prodigy fan since 1996.

'All right, you fuckers, do you want some? Do you want some? I said do
you want some of the fucking Prodigy? Then make some motherfucking
noise.'

As Liam walks across the stage to his rack of keyboards, the crowd
send out a deafening roar. The arena is rammed to the hilt with Prodigy
fans. They go as far back as the stalls and then out to the perimeter. They
stretch as wide as a full one hundred and eighty-degree sweep from the
stage and all of them, every last one, have their hands raised.

The stage is decked out like a futuristic cyber vision of hell. Silver
scaffolding sits in front of a huge backdrop. More bizarrely, the speakers
have spiders clinging to them. Not ordinary spiders though, these
arachnids are ten-foot tall with human heads, all screaming in agony.
It's all very much like the film *Spinal Tap*. And the band know it.

'I just laughed when I first saw them,' says Liam before the gig. 'But
they're cool, aren't they? Kind of tongue-in-cheek.'

The opening drones of The Prodigy's traditional intro of '2001: A
Space Odyssey' fill the night air like an air-raid siren warning of the
carnage that is sure to follow. As the opening break to 'Smack My Bitch
Up' crashes out of the PA, Maxim and Keith run on stage. Maxim in
maroon velvet kilt, hooded furry black and white robe and boxing boots,
Keith in denim jacket with 'British Scooter Club' written on the back, a
long-tailed Union Jack shirt underneath and bleach-stained denim board
shorts. They're a formidable duo. Maxim, the dark lord, flicking his
tongue like a lizard king, rolling his eyes and baring his menacing
silvery-toothed grin; Keith with his hair dyed black and shaped into
rows of spikes, arms outstretched, spinning round like a spring winding
itself up. And when he snaps he becomes a twisted gremlin, a fierce
gargoyle, dribbling insanely at the mouth, staring intensely at the
audience.

The duo are now masters in the art of working a crowd. When Maxim
shouts 'jump!' all you can see is a raging torrent of faces leaping up and
down. Not just in the moshpit at the front either. They go for it as far as
the eye can see.

'We're going to give you one hundred per cent because that's what we
do,' calls Maxim. 'This is going to be the best gig ever . . . I can feel it.'

The crowd surge forward with pure excitement. By the time Liam brings on 'Funky Shit', V97 has turned into a writhing mass of people, moving as one to the beats. Leeroy runs on stage to huge applause, showing off his footwork to the full. His trademark crab-walk shuffle taking him from one side of the stage to the other in five easy strides.

'Breathe' comes in like a runaway juggernaut and the crowd lose it completely. They rush forward, pushing hard to find some space, crushing people at the front in the process. In the photographers' pit the scene is one of complete carnage. Security guards desperately lift people from the crowd, unable to keep up with the continuous stream of injured people who lie strewn across the floor. The first-aid tent directly next to the stage is deluged with fans who have been trampled under foot, overcome by heat or broken limbs under the weight of the shifting movements in the crowd.

Liam sees the mess before him and promptly stops the song. 'Move back or the band won't come back on' commands a security guard over the PA. However the crowd are so tightly packed in that there's nowhere for people to move back to. After almost twenty minutes, people at the back start to leave and the crush eases a little. The band come back on and start up where they left off with 'Breathe'. What follows is the most intense, powerful, angry and adrenalized set the band have played in ages. They run through 'Rock 'n' Roll' (with Leeroy on keyboard duties as Liam takes a rest), 'Serial Thrilla' and 'Their Law' like they're possessed. At the side of the stage, Dave Grohl climbs up the scaffolding to get a better view. He's quickly pursued by security staff. 'Poison' turns into a ten-megaton breakbeat bomb, while 'Firestarter' sends a flame of passion throughout the site, lifting people in a frenzied bout of pogoing. It's as if the band have keyed into the main power supply for Yorkshire and are charged up for the ultimate buzz. V97 in Leeds turns into a gig that will go down in history as one of their best ever. Despite the show-stopping crush that hospitalized three people – with The Prodigy being praised as heroes in the local paper the following day for their quick thinking and unselfish actions.

The following night they take things even further. Playing at the Chelmsford site of the V97 festival, the whole day had the feel of the prodigal son returning. Chelmsford being but a few miles from Braintree, it was as close to a local gig as the band could play.

With the obvious advantage of locality, and the buzz from the night before, The Prodigy played fast and hard, pushing both the audience and themselves to a frenzy. And, unlike the night before, the band weren't forced to abandon the stage mid-song.

'Best gig of the year, no doubt,' enthuses Keith, a grin threatening to take over his entire face. 'It was just a special feeling. The audience, the vibe, everything. Really special.'

'Best gig ever,' adds tour manager John Fairs. 'To see 50,000 people singing along to them tracks, jumping at the same time and chanting back to Maxim, was absolutely fucking amazing.'

Perhaps one of the reasons for the extreme nature of these V97 gigs was down to the simple fact that they'd just returned from another tour of the States which they hadn't particularly enjoyed. As part of the Lollapalooza tour, they visited a string of venues over a three-week period (with a few days off in between to take part in the Mount Fuji Festival in Japan) sharing a bill with artists such as Tool and Tricky. But the crowds weren't as receptive to the Prodigy vibe in the larger arenas. Sure, they went down well, but the atmosphere was flat - despite their album still sitting in the number one slot.

'They just don't get it!' exclaims Maxim. 'This thing has been sitting on their doorstep for ever and they still don't get it. Unless it's got a heavy rock vibe to it. And then they want to know why there isn't a drummer or bassist. It's totally shit.'

'The thing is, Lollapalooza was absolutely shit, a really crap line-up,' adds Liam a week after it had finished. 'We'd been offered a tour with Rage Against the Machine and The Wu Tang Clan at the same time but, because we'd already agreed to Lollapalooza, we had to turn it down. I was gutted about that because I reckon it would have been a much better tour.'

The biggest problem lay with the set up of the venues themselves. With all of the venues seated, the most expensive seats were at the front while further back you could see a moshpit of Prodigy fans who could only afford the cheap seats. It was something which really annoyed the band, not least because they had always stuck by their fans, but also because the stuffed shirts who were occupying the front rows were impossible to vibe off. Not that Keith didn't try his best to do something about it. At times his frustration at the situation was so bad that he jumped into the audience, running up to them, pulling faces, drooling and generally doing what he does best. Each time he did it the promoters went mad, warning him that if he accidentally tripped on someone and they got hurt he would get sued. Keith just ignored the warnings; after all he was as sure-footed as Spiderman and anyway, this kind of behaviour was what they should expect from him. And if they weren't into it they shouldn't have been there in the first place.

Then, one night in Kansas City it happened – some punters threatened to sue him. Not because he'd trampled on them, kicked them or even psychologically damaged them, but because he'd spat water at them! For Keith, spitting water across the audience was a regular and normal part of his performance. However, on this occasion the water he spat happened to land not only on a couple who had only come to see Snoop Doggy Dog (who, incidentally, had finished his set some three hours previously) but it had also gone into a can of Coke one of them was drinking. And to make matters worse, this was no ordinary can of Coke. It had medicine in it for asthma!

Immediately after Keith had projected the offending mix of water and spit into the soft drink, the couple jumped up and started trying to grab him. Keith just shook them off and thought nothing of it. In fact he'd been quite relieved to finally get some kind of reaction. But soon after the show all hell broke loose.

The promoters came into the dressing room saying that the couple wanted to sue Keith. Outside the offended punters were screaming at the tops of their voices, demanding satisfaction. Eventually the band's tour manager John Fairs had to go out and deal with the situation.

'These two were asking for our lawyer's number,' exclaims Leeroy, 'so John's going, "Where was the coke anyway?" and they replied, "On the floor, in the pit." So John just says, "The pit is for the band, not for drinks. You didn't have any authorization to put your drink there." Well, they had to shut up, but they just started going, "We only came for Snoop, your lot are shit." I tell you we don't need people like that. Snoop's welcome to them.'

It turned out to be one of the few truly controversial moments on the tour. The band spent much of the rest of their time shopping, going through the motions of the press schedule and attending the many parties that they were getting invited to. Oh, and then there was the Gizz-baiting which involved constantly having a laugh at their guitarist's expense, and of course, the strip joints. But what do you expect from a bunch of lads on tour in America – regular visits to church?

It was also a time when Maxim grabbed as much space as possible in order to write lyrics for a forthcoming project of his own.

'I had to treat it like I was on holiday, because the monotony of the tour was just getting to me,' admits Maxim. 'I wrote some lyrics, read a couple of books and then did these stupid interviews with local radio stations who didn't have a clue what we were about. They'd be saying, "So you're the drummer." I'm like, "No, I'm the guitarist," know what I mean? I tell you it was getting to be a bit of a pain.'

It was on 20 July while in Columbus, Ohio, on the first date of the tour, that the *NME* reported on Maxim's shopping habits while on tour. Returning from a quick shopping expedition, the journalists noted that he was clutching a bag crammed with white Tommy Hilfiger boxer shorts.

'It's not the kind of thing I wear normally,' he says, 'but you have to be careful when you're wearing a kilt on stage and you've got the whole world's photographers in the pit underneath you! You can't wear a pair of crusty old Y-fronts, can you?'

And this was just about as rock'n'roll as things got on the entire tour.

The following night in Cincinnati, Maxim came face to face with one of the regular phenomenons that dog the band wherever they go. It's called the 'I'm English, ain't I?' syndrome. And Maxim and Keith stare it in the face at regular intervals while on foreign trips.

Essentially, the syndrome happens whenever the vocalists climb into the pit and go up to the audience. What normally ensues is a lot of shouting, laughing and maybe a bit of playful jostling. Invariably, however, the front row are too in awe of Maxim's demonic stares and continuous speaking in silent tongues, and Keith's drooling, alien grin, to react in any way other than stunned amazement. Nevertheless, every time the band hit a foreign land there's an English bloke amongst the front rows with a huge grin and shouting louder than anyone else.

'I tell you, it don't matter where we are, there's always matey down there shouting "English, me" while pointing at himself,' exclaims Keith. 'Of course it's a different geezer every time but it might as well not be. Matey's always going, "I'm from Darlington" or wherever, like I'm supposed to suddenly hug him like my long-lost brother.'

In Cincinnati this syndrome goes beyond the usual banter. About half-way thorough the set, Maxim went off on a rare walk into the audience, in an attempt to vibe things up a bit. As he ran towards the cheaper seats where the moshing was going, one bloke started gesticulating wildly for Maxim to go up to him. Unusually, he actually did, but this bloke wasn't your ordinary punter, he seemed slightly more animated that the others. Maxim leant over the barrier, tongue flicking like Kaa from *The Jungle Book*, eyes rolling like a psycho and then just stared at the guy who'd been shouting to him. What Maxim was to hear next he just couldn't believe. The shouting man only offered to sell him some Ecstasy!

'This geezer gets me and goes "sorted?" As if I'm going to say, "Mate, you've saved the day. I'll just get you some money out of my back pocket and score off you now, shall I? Hang on, I'll just ask the rest of the band as well, don't go away though, will you?" It just makes you laugh that people reckon that offering us drugs is the way to become our mate.'

Much to the disbelief of many people, The Prodigy's drug intake had by now been all but eradicated. They hadn't taken Ecstasy since their early days and even the dope was becoming a rarity among the group. Well . . . they didn't smoke anything like as much as they used to.

Maxim explains, 'We're not like the average group. The amount of energy that we put into each gig means that we can't do drugs. If we did, we wouldn't be able to give it our one hundred per cent. But people always reckon we're on drugs. I'm actually the straightest member of the band, I don't smoke any more, I only drink maybe two glasses of wine after the gig. I don't even go out much at home. I maybe get pissed up and go out and have a fight every couple of months to get it out of my system, know what I mean? But people still think I'm totally wired on stage. But when I'm performing I couldn't go on stage pissed or stoned. It would just take that edge away.'

Following the next gig on 23 July in Indianapolis, The Prodigy bailed out of Lollapalooza for a three-day trip to Japan.

The band were booked to play at the annual Mount Fuji festival alongside many of the bands they'd been playing with continuously over the last three years. Rage Against the Machine, Red Hot Chili Peppers, Beck; all of the usual suspects had been lined up to play in one of the most spectacular locations the international rock calender can offer.

Playing in a green valley beneath the snow-capped mountain, it offers a picture of tranquillity; except for the stages and the endless line-up of bands from around the world. The Mount Fuji Festival is a paragon of organization. People are bussed into the location, their tickets are checked with the utmost efficiency and speed, whilst the stage management itself runs like clockwork, each changeover handled swiftly and with the absolute minimum of fuss.

The security is second to none, too. There's no blagging your way past the Japanese guards who stand by the backstage entrance. Without the correct pass you could be the lead singer in the headlining band and you still wouldn't get in. Backstage being strictly limited to band and crew only, this is one festival which doesn't turn into an industry schmooze from beginning to end. Which in itself is quite refreshing.

The crowd themselves are also another matter entirely. Despite years of travelling to Western countries, buying up sub-cultures by the bucketload, that Japanese reserve refuses to go away. So despite an audience dressed in their finest skate gear, their best B-boy cool or their spot-on interpretation of the LA surf dude, they still find it hard to lose themselves in the music.

No stage diving here, certainly no throwing of mud, cans or whatever else usually comes to hand. At the Mount Fuji festival the kids dance politely, apologize when they knock into someone when they're slam dancing and wait until the very end of each song to applaud. But there's no denying that they absolutely love the music, as much as anyone anywhere in the world, and, as the first day sees the Chili Peppers deliver a brilliant set to an enthusiastic crowd, The Prodigy start to get excited about their appearance the following night.

Japan has always been one of The Prodigy's favourite destinations. Ever since the arse-photocopying episode a few years back, they've looked forward to Japanese dates with relish. The shopping's great, the people are polite and it gives them a chance to let off steam without the prying eyes of English journalists reporting everything back.

Letting off steam means sessions in the karaoke bars, sinking more than their collective body weight in tequila. It involves being slightly leery – louder than the locals anyway – and performing the usual high pranks.

Japan has long held a huge respect for The Prodigy too. Both *Experience* and *Music for the Jilted Generation* were released there to huge acclaim, the Japanese instantly on the wavelength of Liam's fascination for a multitude of different sub-cultures and their associated genres. Furthermore, the band's singles have all been released in Japan as mixed collections, which bring together every track available in the UK and fuse them together in a continuous DJ set. As such, these albums have become highly collectible, with English bootleggers turning round copies by the truckload.

On the morning of their gig, the band looked out from their hotel rooms to see the kind of weather they'd only ever seen on television. Overnight a typhoon had swept inland bringing with it unbelievably high winds and torrential rain. They'd been told the night before that there was a chance of a typhoon coming their way but the band had just shrugged it off. After all, in Japan, typhoon and earthquake warnings were as regular as breakfast.

This typhoon was far more than just a warning, however. As it ripped through the festival sight it cut the power, weakened the stage and generally turned the place into a disaster site. The gig had to be cancelled. It was 27 July and they weren't due to return to Kansas City, the US, for two days. What could they do? The question wasn't on their lips for long. Having retired to the bar to discuss alternative plans, they started on a drinking session which was to last for the rest of their stay.

However, one person in the band did get to perform: Keith. On the band's first night in Japan they had gone to check out Rage Against the Machine playing in a club. Towards the end of the set, vocalist Zack de la Rocha invited Keith on stage. Naturally he went for it with the usual energy, bringing the house down (in the Japanese way) in the process.

When the band returned to the US there was a distinct difference in the crowds. The first three dates had seen only half-full halls with subdued audiences. It was a fact which forced a rumour that the tour was going to be aborted due to its loss-making situation. Indeed, even before the tour had started out, bands like Jon Spencer's Blues Explosion had allegedly been forced to pull out because their initial fee had been sliced in half, thus making it economically impossible for them to play.

While The Prodigy had been sinking Japan's annual supply of tequila, something had happened stateside. The tickets had suddenly started flying out. Demand had literally gone through the roof almost overnight. As a result when the band returned they came face to face with sell-out crowds, all going mad for them. The reason? The album had been out a couple of weeks and demand at last had gone beyond their hardcore following. Suddenly, middle America was falling for The Prodigy sonic equation.

From here on in the band rocked through St Louis on the 30th and Nashville Tennessee on the 31st. August was ushered in with Dallas on the 2nd while the following night they played at Corpus Christi, Arizona. Despite the growing popularity of the band, this tour was far from being the most enjoyable, with the press and punters alike still finding it hard to understand how a geezer behind some keyboards, two dancers (one with a microphone), and an MC, could possibly constitute a band.

'I couldn't believe it, they were still saying, "Where's your drummer?" You know what I mean?' says Leeroy. Each day brought with it even more dumb questions from local radio DJs who seemed far more interested in getting the band to record idents for them. How many times Liam, Leeroy, Maxim and Keith must have said, 'Hi, we're The Prodigy and we listen to . . . what's the station called again?' was beyond belief. America was turning into something of an exercise in keeping cool and testing their stamina.

On 3 August disaster struck for Leeroy. The band were playing in Corpus Christi, deep inside Texas, when Leeroy strained a ligament, leaving him in intense pain and barely able to hobble off the stage. Three nights later the band were due to play Phoenix, Arizona ('the most boring place in the world' was the band's official statement). The temperature was at an incredible 110 degrees and Leeroy's leg was still in a bad way. He was forced to do something he hadn't done in seven years; pull out of the gig.

'Well gutted' was Leeroy's reaction. 'I've played gigs with the flu, when I've had stomach bugs – I even played when I broke my arm [following a snowboarding accident], I just went on with my arm in plaster. But my leg just wouldn't have taken the strain.'

Leeroy wasn't to miss the gig totally though. For a long time, Liam had used 'Rock and Roll' for a quick break from the keyboards. Initially it allowed him space to play drums, latterly it just gave him a chance to get his breath back and have a quick drink. At this point, Leeroy usually took over on keyboard duties.

'Liam's like, "You're still going to do 'Rock and Roll', aren't you? I need the rest,"' explains Leeroy. 'The thing is, Liam suffers loads in the heat. Actually it's because he's got a bit of a fitness situation, he can't even touch his own toes. Have you noticed the gut he's getting?'

Sure enough, Liam came off stage during 'Rock and Roll', leaving Leeroy to limp up into the keyboard riser. But seeing the rest of the show was to open Leeroy's eyes to another side of The Prodigy. For the first time ever he could see what the fans saw.

'I just had tears in my eyes,' he recalls a few weeks later. 'It just hit me what an amazing band The Prodigy really are. And the weirdest thing was I could even imagine what I look like on stage when my songs were playing. It was like I was seeing myself up there. Like I said, I had tears in my eyes.'

Leeroy was seeing what millions of people world-wide had known for some time – The Prodigy were one of the most exciting propositions in the live arena and with albums to match they were indeed that rare breed, a band who could cut it just as well in the studio as they could on stage.

In the middle of the Lollapalooza tour 'Breathe' was finally released in America. The demand for it was said to be going through the roof, as MTV had played the video constantly. The industry expected great things from the single, hoping that it would emulate the album and reach the top slot in the Billboard Chart. In the end, it barely managed to scrape into the top fifty. The record label was in turmoil, while some of the UK papers reported it as some kind of triumph of common sense.

The reason for the poor showing, it was discovered, had little to do with actual sales but more to do with how radio playlists are compiled. A random cross-section of people are played snippets of tracks over the phone and asked if they want to hear more. Unfortunately, the raw tones of 'Breathe' were a little too much for the average American, and, as a result, The Prodigy's votes were relatively low. Consequently they gained hardly any radio air-play, which badly affected the single's showing in the charts. It would seem that in order to get to number one in this particular chart The Prodigy would have to turn into Michael Bolton – which, let's face it, isn't likely.

After the ups and downs of America and Japan, followed by their amazing homecoming performances at V97, the band headed off to Scotland and Ireland to continue sharing The Prodigy experience. The Scottish date at Glasgow Green on 23 August took place in front of 100,000 people, all singing in unison to the opening track: '*Change my pitch up, smack my bitch up.*' And if that wasn't amazing enough, the crowd even sang along to the Indian chant in the middle of the song.

'It's like something you can't descibe, to hear that,' enthuses Leeroy a couple of days later. 'To hear people singing along, it's like . . . fucking out of this world. I'm still shell-shocked.'

The following day, at the Trip to Tip festival in Ireland, the show was equally enthralling, although one thing stood out above all else: the huge amount of people dressed just like Keith. It was a phenomenon which had first become obvious at the V97 gigs, but here there were thousands of people with their hair shaved down the middle, dyed multi-coloured either side and gelled into spikes. In some cases they'd even copied Keith's stage outfit, and sported Union Jack tail shirts and bondage denims with beer-mat bum flaps.

Clearly the Keith image had turned into a monster.

* * * * *

'I haven't told anyone else this, but at the moment I'm not doing another album.'

Liam, May 1997

Just before the release of *The Fat of the Land*, Liam came out with this extraordinary statement while we were, in a manner of speaking, chewing the fat over the album. In many ways it was a statement which could have been a shock. If I'd been in any way surprised I probably would have got in touch immediately with one of the papers I write for to sell the story. It was, after all, a scoop.

However a little research would show that this wasn't the first time Liam had made such a claim. In March 1995, Liam told *NME*'s Iestyn George that, '. . . I've told the label that I'm not even going to do another album unless I come up with something special.' In the cut-throat world of the media this quote could have been interpreted as declaring that *Music for the Jilted Generation* was to be the band's last album. Indeed it would have been interpreted as such if they'd had a single like 'Firestarter' out. But at that time The Prodigy weren't famous enough, so the quote went over people's heads.

In 1997 it was a different matter. Liam calling it quits was big news. But listening to the rest of what he had to say made things far clearer. This wasn't the end of The Prodigy, just a way for Liam to close the door on one adventure and start looking toward the next.

'I never think about the future; what we're gonna be doing in another year,' he continues. 'This is enough to be getting on with at the moment. The band will continue as long as we're progressing. There's no way I sit down and start thinking when should I start writing the next album?'

Two months later *Select* magazine ran their interview with the band. The shock headline? 'This is our last album!' Liam had repeated the same statement that I'd heard to the *Select* reporter. Unfortunately the reporter hadn't listened to the rest of what Liam was saying. Or perhaps he did listen, but the shock retirement statement, alongside the band dressed in natty suits à la Blues Brothers (but intended to be in honour of two-tone) was guaranteed to sell issues of the magazine in droves. So what had prompted such a quote? Probably the journalist's question was the same as mine had been back in Liam's front room: 'Whats next, Liam? What are your plans for the future?'

It doesn't take too much detective work to realize that Liam's thoughts have been increasingly drawn back to his hip hop roots. The breakbeats of *The Fat of the Land* are just one of the giveaways. Another clue lies in the tracks hidden away on the B-sides of 'Firestarter' and 'Breathe'. Firstly, 'Molotov Bitch' displayed just how much Liam has been an influence on the big beat scene. Back when he was churning out breakbeat tunes for his first album, Liam came under a lot of criticism from the techno scene. The breakbeat was considered to be the tool of the hardcore raver and, as a result, no longer found a home in the underground. A number of years later when Liam released 'Poison', the underground dance scene had moved onto house music and therefore rejected The Prodigy's latest breakbeat sound.

Yet there was also a group of producers who had grown out of the same scene as Liam, who'd always loved hip hop and who also declared a love for guitar music. Artists like The Chemical Brothers took the blueprint from The Prodigy and ran with it, eventually turning the sound into what it is today. With 'Molotov Bitch', however, Liam had merely pushed the ideas displayed in 'Poison' and made them harder faster and more in your face. The end result was as big as any of the big beat tunes.

'The Trick', which appeared on the flip-side of 'Breathe', saw Liam returning to his B-boy roots, with an instrumental hip hop number which hints massively at the sound of The Wu Tang Clan. Of course, it was 'Release Yo' Delf', his Method Man remix, which had fully re-aligned Liam with the beats of hip hop and, as he moves onto the next stage of The Prodigy's development, it seems certain that this rekindled love will play a major part.

'There are a few slower tunes which I was working on during the recording of this album that I'd like to return to,' admits Liam. 'They're fucking wicked, really good tunes but they weren't quite ready. I've even been thinking about doing a whole load of hip hop tunes like that Method Man remix. I could knock those off in my sleep!'

With the success of his Method Man remix, it comes as no surprise that Liam has recently been approached to remix no fewer than four tracks off the man's forthcoming album. Furthermore, he's been approached to remix a couple of Wu Tang Clan tracks. The latter is a particular honour as not only is Liam a huge fan of theirs but also he's the only person they're approaching to do the task.

Beyond the hip hop vibe, there are also plans afoot to extend the working relationship with Rage Against the Machine. Following the extremely fruitful pairing of Liam and guitarist Tom Morello, the pair talked, during the Japanese break in the Lollapalooza tour, about the possibility of doing an entire album together.

'The thing with that track was that I really wanted to do it, but it was rushed in the end. It took three days, so it's really fucking direct. That vocal on it was a last-minute decision but he loved it . . . he was really fucking into it. We talked loads in Japan and he was going, "Yeah man, we'll do loads of tracks."'

The idea of collaborating with artists from diverse fields also fills Liam with excitement. He has often expressed an interest in working with Dave Grohl of The Foo Fighters, and Grohl has returned the compliment. If Grohl's scaffold-climbing behaviour at V97 (just to get a better view of The Prodigy) is anything to go by, this pairing should happen sooner rather than later.

As for The Prodigy, well, it stands to reason that there'll be another album. As Liam says, he only stated that *The Fat of the Land* was the last album as his way of coping with the pressure of the situation. Unusually, however, much of the pressure was down to his own perfectionist nature. There were a number of tracks which didn't make it onto the album because they simply didn't fit into the jigsaw. Indeed prior to 'Serial Thrilla', Liam and Keith had been working on a dubby track which, although they liked it, didn't quite fit with the vibe Liam wanted.

In fact, if it came to it, there would be a pretty good album of out-takes, which the band have continued to perform live. Cuts like 'Rock and Roll', a huge crowd favourite which has yet to make it onto CD. Or tracks like 'Acid Break', 'Gabba' and 'Come Correct', which have constantly appeared in the band's live shows over the past two years. However with Liam's need to keep things tight, it's hardly likely that these tracks will see the light of day in any way other than B-sides.

Beyond any notion of an album there are the other potential singles from *The Fat of the Land*. First up is 'Smack My Bitch Up' which has had remixes done by label-mate Jonny L and junglist DJ Hype, apparently simply for the money! However given Hype's own Essex roots and rave past it's probably more likely that the mixes have also been done out of respect as well.

The release of 'Smack My Bitch Up' would appear to be little short of commercial suicide for The Prodigy right now. Riding high with the album, this return to their roots might alienate people who have recently discovered the band. Furthermore, the controversial nature of Kool Keith's vocal line will undoubtedly get a huge roar of disapproval from the greater media.

On the other hand, it would make perfect sense for the single to come out now. As Liam, and indeed the whole band have said, they don't want to be famous and they certainly don't want to be seen as one of the biggest bands in the world, and it wouldn't bother them in the least if this single doesn't go straight in at number one. A track which ties so heavily into their underground ideologies would remind the country what they're about at a time when they've become perceived as the band with the strange clown in it. As hundreds of young people continue to dress like Keith, it would be a timely reminder that The Prodigy are an alternative dance band without one single frontman.

The other proposed single is 'Serial Thrilla', although Liam doesn't count out the possibility of 'Mindfields'.

'Both are really good tracks,' he declares. 'I'd love to do a remix of "Serial Thrilla" to give it more edge and I've already got "Mindfields" sorted, with a version which I think is better than the album.'

As for recording a new album, Liam insists that there will be one. It's just that he doesn't know when. One change he will make to the recording process, however, will be to bring in another engineer to work on the time-consuming stuff. Working in this way would free Liam up to concentrate on writing the tunes. A process which only comes into fruition when he's satisfied.

'Every time I go in the studio I want to shock myself and if that don't happen, nothing happens.'

For the rest of the band, 1998 looks like it will be the year when they step out into the world of songwriting in their own right. Much of the talk is currently about the band having a Wu Tang Clan vibe in which the various members of the band can go off and create their own solo material before returning to the fold of the mothership band.

To this end, Maxim has already secured a deal with XL Records for his own album, to be released in June 1998. Much of the material is heavily hip hop based with a huge Parliament and Funkadelic influence. The project also features Maxim delivering full lyrics, although there will doubtless be quite a few surprises as well. Indeed, Maxim has been penning lyrics for the project throughout 1997.

It's no surprise that Maxim has started on his own musical venture. Although he goes to great lengths to underline the fact that The Prodigy is still his main thing, this solo project is very much a hangover from his days prior to the band. Back then he was actively involved in the process of writing music and, despite having occasional outlets for his lyricism with Liam, he still gets frustrated at times. Recording the material is his way of letting go of this frustration. It allows him the chance to explore creative sides of himself which have lain dormant over the last six years.

Working in his own home studio, Maxim is able to go down far funkier roads than The Prodigy will travel. His great loves being funk, hip hop and of course the old soundsystem sounds of reggae with which he first discovered his lyrical talent. The Maxim album moves through the whole range, allowing him to deliver varying vocal styles. In fact, at times his vocals are almost completely different to those with which he MCs in The Prodigy.

The extent to which this venture will take up Maxim's time is still unknown, but since the band have only a handful of dates confirmed through the early part of 1998, it means that he will have the space to promote the album. Playing live with it is still pretty much unlikely, though.

The person one might think least likely to get into a musical project is Leeroy. As a dancer who, in Liam's words, 'has yet to find his voice', Leeroy has often been portrayed as the non-musical side of the band. Surprisingly he was the first person out of 'the other three' to release a record in his own right.

Going under the name of The Longman, he sneakily put out a white label single in August 1996. Essentially a breakbeat-based affair with flourishes of old skool electro, the single moves into much funkier terrain than The Prodigy's material. It's also a record which betrays Leeroy's breakdancing roots.

Working as The Longman, Leeroy has already had one of his tracks included on the Kiss compilation, *Needs Must*, released in early 1997. Beyond this, he has also supplied a remix for an as-yet unreleased Shades of Rhythm single.

'They're all like local to us so I've known them for ages,' explains the Longman himself. 'So they gave me this electro track to remix and I really enjoyed it. I especially enjoyed it on a technical level, which is where I think me and Liam differ in our ways of working. I like to get into the finer intricacies of the software. I'll sit there and learn the manual inside out, whereas Liam's much more direct. I think it's because he's the artist and me . . . well, I was an electrician.'

Although Leeroy's musical ability may already have been utilized by Liam during the live rendition of 'Rock and Roll', with Leeroy's increasingly in-depth knowledge as a studio engineer and Liam's need for someone to do the practical work in the studio, perhaps the duo may end up working together on recording tracks for The Prodigy.

Whatever happens, Leeroy has already started laying down tracks for a forthcoming single and insists that he's got more than enough ideas for a 'damn funky album'.

'The main problem at the moment is finding time,' he laments, 'but as soon as I do I'll be straight in the studio to sort it out. I'm actually trying to buy a new place at the moment so I can build my own studio.'

With a deal currently under negotiation, Leeroy doesn't expect the first fruits of his labour to see the light of day until at least mid 1998. He's in no hurry; after all, The Prodigy is still his main thing.

Which leaves Keith, a man who not only found his voice when Liam wrote 'Firestarter' but who has also discovered his own distinct form of lyricism. Since then he has constantly been scribbling down words for his own venture, although at the moment he has no idea what this might be. Given Keith's love of American punk rock it's probably a safe bet that, unlike the others, his side project will involve real musicians. But then again, Keith is a man who constantly surprises, so who knows, he may well come out with a Pink Floydesque journey through the many moods and experiences that feature in his life. He undoubtedly has the ideas and talent. Whatever the case, it's sure to be an extreme project which will strip the paint off a passing exocet missile!

Howevere, there is one thing in the pipeline for Keith that doesn't involve making music. His first acting part! Friends of the band's, as Mad Dog Productions, are to make a film late in 1997, which will feature none other than our Flinty acting the part of a newsreader. Your Oscar awaits, sir!

With such solo projects going on, the press usually start to cry, 'they've split!' This was something which actually affected Leeroy back when his Longman EP came out. People put that together with the fact that since Keith's increased vocal role, Leeroy has had fewer tunes to dance to in the Prodigy set. The rumour quickly started to circulate that he was getting sick of the band and was thinking of quitting.

'A load of crap,' insists Leeroy. 'It's never entered my mind to give up The Prodigy. This is my main thing and I love it. That's why I did The Longman as such a low-profile thing . . . because I knew people would start saying that I was going to leave.'

This is doubtless something which the others will be forced to face up to in the very near future, however all four of them insist that The Prodigy is still very much a band . . . and it will stay that way until the day it becomes boring.

Any plans for solo projects would of course have to wait until after The Prodigy had finalized their dates promoting *The Fat of the Land*. Given the amount of gigging the band do, this could mean waiting a very long time. On 19 August 1997 The Prodigy announced their final UK dates of the year. From 6 December their tour takes them through a series of dates in medium-sized venues around the country.

Given the popularity of the band, they could easily have played in the larger arena-sized venues and still sold out in ten minutes flat, but Liam was opposed to this idea.

'The promoters were saying that we should do the stadiums this time but I was totally against it. I don't want it to go that big because we're not a stadium band – we still like the closeness of smaller venues. That's why we're thinking of doing some secret gigs just before the tour. We saw The Red Hot Chili Peppers play at Subterranea in London last year and it was fucking amazing. That's the kind of thing we'd like to do. Set up a few secret shows, just for the buzz, so we can maybe play around a bit and not have to do a straight set.'

Prior to these UK shows, the band are once again off to play in Russia, despite declaring that they would never again go there. The show is part of a three-country tour which the band were determined to do, not because of the money or even the prestige, but because the shows are part of a European snowboarding festival.

What a perfect way to kill two birds with one stone. Playing live at night, snowboarding by day . . .

'Hey, it's not all fast cars, fast women and loads of drink you know,' laughs Keith. 'Sometimes we have to work really hard and anyway we're usually the first to be back at the hotel and tucked up in bed. Nah, mate, we're just not yer rock'n'roll types.'

True, Keith. You're not straight-faced, you don't take yourselves too seriously and, above all, you're not arrogant idiots who are constantly fighting. You're definitely not rock'n'roll types – you're much more than that.

*   *   *   *   *

We really don't consider ourselves as being of a size any more, we've switched off from thinking about how big we're getting. All we say now is 'did it rock?' and if it did it's mission completed and we're happy. If you get on stage and you get like a raging north Atlantic sea in front of you, that is all your rewards. A lot of bands, especially from where we were coming from, wouldn't play in places that were out of the way. You know, like some of the really smaller places and countries that we've been to. But we did and people were like, 'Shit, we don't get many bands here,' which really stumped us. But we went there, it rocked, we got the right reaction and we owe it to those people to go back there again.

Keith, June 1997

They are easily the most important band this country has produced in the past five years. Oasis may sell well and be huge in Britain, but they sound so English. The Prodigy have a truly international appeal.

Daniel Miller, Mute Records (who licensed Music for the Jilted Generation in the US) in Music Week, June 1997

There's little doubt that The Prodigy are a band for whom the word adventure was created, their endless touring giving way to a multitude of episodes of wild and laddish behaviour. But what is it that makes them so special? Why The Prodigy?

Looking back over six years of press coverage, one thing that immediately strikes you is the way journalists have gone overboard with exaggerated superlatives. They've been described as everything from 'Beztastic cartoon ravers with bonkers tunes' to 'the best rock'n'roll band in the world'. They've been written about with the kind of familiarity which verges on disrespect, barely hiding the fact that in 1997, despite the band's huge success on a record-breaking world-wide scale, the indie-centric music press still don't take them seriously, while the dance press seemingly still can't forgive them for moving on from the clubs.

Witness the way *Mixmag* highlighted Liam's claims that he hated house music on the cover line for their July 1997 issue. As if that was a surprise to anyone who had followed the band? Witness the reviews of The Prodigy's disastrous power cut at Glastonbury which failed to put the torrential rain in the circuits down to *force majeure*, or an act of God, instead it was the band's fault. They were blamed for not letting the crowd know what was going on, as if, in the absence of the music they were supposed to turn into a public announcement team. 'Ladies and gentlemen, The Prodigy will now be taking a twenty-minute break while we get the hair dryer on those wet parts.' It just doesn't cut it, does it?

Nevertheless, the following week the music industry was rife with rumours as to why the power had cut. The rain long forgotten, in its place came the suggestion that Liam was running sub-standard, old and indeed cheap gear. The proof was, apparently, in the fact that the machinery had broken down a couple of times in Europe as well. According to some sources, Liam had earned the nickname 'How much?' Howlett because his reaction to the suggestion that he upgraded his gear was always met with that same response.

The Prodigy have never quite fitted into the neat packages that the media industry require. They haven't sat easily with journalists who like their bands to be real and their rock stars to be sullen and argumentative. The Prodigy aren't like this. They're mates, they have a laugh and they don't wash their dirty linen in public – if indeed there is any. They just get on with having a great time and doing what they do until someone finally pulls the plug on their show for good.

Many sections of the media still present them as dodgy old ravers, as if that in some way implies that the Ecstasy has taken away their personalities and the music that Liam creates isn't in any way worthy of critical attention. Sure, they'll be put on front cover after front cover, but rarely has anyone taken the time to probe into the make-up of the band despite their obvious attributes. No-one, it seems, is prepared to take them seriously.

The Fat of the Land was the fastest selling album in the UK ever. It went straight in to the number one slots all over the world and as such became one of Britain's hottest properties. But, when the Spice Girls went to number one in the US, the fact was met with a far greater response from every form of media in Britain. When Oasis's third album *Be Here Now* was released the excitement surrounding its arrival made it onto the national TV news, which followed up the story only a week later with news that it had become the fastest-selling album in the UK since their last album. In so doing, The Prodigy's record was suddenly written out of the history books. But why? Why wasn't the equally feverish clamour to buy *The Fat of the Land* worthy of television cameras, why was the band's popularity in the rest of the world all but ignored? The Prodigy's standing must surely be as one of the biggest bands in the world, yet they're still treated like flash-in-the-pan upstarts. Ironically it's a situation which Liam likes.

'Look, we've got no intention of being as popular as Oasis or The Spice Girls. Why would we? I mean my dad likes Oasis, and I don't want to make music that my dad and his mates will like. That's just not what The Prodigy is about. I want to write the kind of music that people complain about . . . "turn that bloody noise down", you know what I mean?'

This deliberately subversive stance has meant that it hasn't been easy to assimilate The Prodigy into the given scheme of things. They are outsiders, and that's one of the things which is so appealing about them.

Another thing which immediately separates them from the other bands around, is their difference. At a time when the majority of bands are judged on their similarity, The Prodigy are unique. At no point can you say that they've ripped off The Beatles or The Rolling Stones, or whoever best represents the week's most fashionable era. Despite this, it has become commonplace for criticism to be levelled at Liam for his appropriation of other people's music in the form of sampling.

Liam's art isn't simply to lift, however. What he does is sample, deconstruct and rearrange. The sound of the sample becomes an instrument in itself, which is adjusted to become an intrinsic part of the track in some way. Despite samplers having been in general use for more than a decade, their use is still regarded in many circles as being in some way non-musical. The source, though, is hailed as the pure form, a fact which has a lot to do with the retro nature of popular culture as we reach the end of the millennium. 'Spotting the sample' carries with it the kind of snobbery that record trainspotting achieves.

If the skill of sampling is to be regarded as a science rather than an art form then many of today's most retro bands should surely be condemned with it. Artists like Oasis, Blur and Cast, along with many others, have built their careers on assimilating the entire sound of older, mainstream artists. Not only that but they employ the very same technology that Liam uses to record his own music. Listen closely to one of the above artists albums and you will hear the sample running alongside the click track. Yet, because Liam's music is so obviously created on machinery, it's instantly removed from the rock'n'roll heritage and placed directly into the much younger history of electronic music.

The beauty of The Prodigy is that their music is as much from one heritage as the other. As Leeroy says about '3 Kilos', from the bands second album *Music for the Jilted Generation*:

'If you were to take that and press it onto a seven-inch, put a knackered old white label on it and then rub it gently with light sandpaper to scratch it up a bit, nobody would know it wasn't a 1960s track. But it doesn't sound like anyone in particular from the 1960s. It's just got a vibe. That's what's brilliant about Liam's music, he can create that vibe using any sound he wants.'

This idea of tapping into the vibe of a time is perhaps the most alien thing to the musical mainstream. The vibe is an abstract force which is defined by ambience and attitudes rather than the concrete ideals of personality and critique. The vibe is something which remains central to the mind set of the rave generation as they've grown up and moved to pastures new. It has remained central to The Prodigy's ideology and, as such, it has in many ways become more important than the individuals themselves. Sure, their individuality has been presented in videos and on stage, but this individuality still sits directly within the framework of the vibe. Keith, the all-or-nothing personality moving from incredibly gentle to terrifyingly fierce in matter of seconds, riding on the energy of that vibe; Maxim, one minute laid back, the next staring with the eyes of the devil; and Leeroy painting pictures with his body, writing poetry with his moves – all through the vibes created by the vibe-master Liam Howlett.

This attitude to the vibe is one which also separates the band from their roots in club culture. Where once the abstract force was paramount to the rave energy, by 1997 a different star system had been introduced into the scene. The vibe had been assimilated into the culture as a marketable force and the music itself had become divided into fragmented sub-genres, each aimed at certain DJs. It's a scene where creativity is increasingly suffocated at the expense of the DJs' mixing abilities, and talents like Liam would thus find it incredibly difficult to come through on the same scale. When Liam dropped 'What Evil Lurks' back in 1991, he was representing the whole scene, the entire attitude, not just the particular style of one or two DJs.

In 1997 The Prodigy still represent a particular mind set. However this time it's based around peculiarly eclectic times. Eclecticism is an ideology which any number of musicians have adhered to over recent years. Many critics might have claimed that it's part of the pre-millenial condition, a by-product of chaotic times. The Prodigy would simply say that they've been influenced by the things they've seen over the course of the last few years. However it must also be said that The Prodigy's huge popularity has come at a time when, much to the dismay of the world's marketing men, people are rejecting the tidy niches of genre and discovering a wide range of tastes.

For anyone who grew up through the rave times, but still listened to *Screamadelica* by Primal Scream, anything by Happy Mondays and the first album by The Stone Roses, it's impossible not to have been affected by a huge pot pourri of musical styles: rock, hip hop, dub, reggae, funk, techno – all of them represented by the music of the times. The direct result of this was an initial attempt by the industry to push the purist form of 'Brit pop'. However the rave-generation artists had already unleashed the idea that it didn't matter what you listened to, it didn't matter what era it came from, as long as it was quality. As the effects of this have been carried into the next generation, the record buying public have rejected the concept that says they should be only one type of person; that they can only listen to indie, dance, hip hop or whatever. Today people listen to what they like.

It's this anti-marketability which The Prodigy tap into. The public can instantly see that they haven't been created. They immediately know that the band do their own thing and as such they have come to represent some of the things that people like in their heroes. Once again The Prodigy are outsiders. And at a time when a great many people feel in some way disenfranchized from their own society (thanks to the previous government's draconian, anti-party legislation and policies concerning benefits for young people, and the current government's pay-for-your-own-education policy), The Prodigy seem to encompass that feeling of living on the edge of the perception of what's acceptable. The Prodigy have come to be the spokespeople for that jilted generation. And what do they say? Live your life to the full, do what you want to do and experience as much as you can.

Unlike any other band around at the moment, The Prodigy are a unit. If any one member of the band quit it would be impossible for The Prodigy to carry on, unlike many others who change their drummers and bassists as often as the seasons. It's a testament to Liam that he has allowed his musical vision to become a vehicle for three other personalities. It's a testament to Keith, Leeroy and Maxim, however, that they've become so important to Liam's musical process that to separate them would mean the death of the band.

The Prodigy are like a jigsaw. Their personalities interlink to create a whole. Liam is quiet, almost shy, but with a dry wit which can cut people down as soon as they walk into the room. It's through the others he has been able to come out of himself and express the things which for a long time had remained hidden inside his own mind. His apparently serious nature (although in the privacy of the band and friends he lightens up considerably) betrays a man who feels a kind of responsibility to the others, and they look to him for directions. Maxim is similarly quiet. However his almost aloof appearance isn't down to any form of shyness. He's a thinker, someone who likes to weigh up situations rather than just blunder in. Not scared, perhaps a little cynical, but certainly self-protective in his caution. His maturity, along with his natural *joi de vivre*, imbues the others with a calmness that's essential to their keeping their heads together. Keith, the double-edged personality whose hyperactivity coupled with his chilled other side, makes him the wild card in the pack. It's a necessary energy that the others need as much as does Keith himself. Leeroy is the joker, the cathartic release for the tensions that the others feel. But he's also the rock that keeps them steady. Liam describes Leeroy as 'the mother' in the band. He's the person who fixes things when they're going a little wrong.

Together, The Prodigy are more than just a band, they're a gang. And not simply a gang that you want to join, but a gang you feel part of when you see them play or listen to their records. The Voodoo crew extends way beyond those people on stage. It's a fellowship of people who also live for the buzz, the vibe, the energy and the experience.

That The Prodigy are now in the position to afford more, do more and experience more, is almost irrelevant because they remain rebellious in a way that belies their chart status. You can't imagine Keith hanging around with the Prime Minister of Britain, sharing tea and sandwiches.

But you can imagine them hanging out with the great rebels of rock music: Johnny Rotten, David Bowie et al. You can't imagine The Prodigy arguing about who was going to sing the next song on the album, but you can imagine them arguing about who would get the chance to test drive a new sports car. And, despite the band's celebrity status, they're still a part of the greater vibe and thus in complete unity with their audience - the jilted generation, the Voodoo crew.

None of this would have been possible without Liam's music in the first place. Indeed, the music itself acts as a microcosm of the psychological make-up of the whole band. It's simple, direct music. Easy to understand and quick to get into. But this doesn't mean that it's in any way stupid music. An assumption which is far too easy to make. Listening to their entire back catalogue you discover that although each record is most definitely of its time, within the track itself lies an undercurrent of musical rebellion. The songs don't do what they're supposed to do within the restrictions of the genre. Scratch beneath the surface of the material on *Experience* for instance, and you find ideas running through it which are at complete odds with the rest of the dance or rave scene that surrounded it at the time. The loops are much more raw, the sequences amazingly simple, yet often going against the structure of the track. 'Charly', for example, may have seemed like a novelty tune to a lot of people, but take away the cat sample and what you have is a hard and dark breakbeat track which found Liam already defining his own rules for making music. The cut-ups of the breaks were completely out on a limb from the rest of the scene, while the bass line came from a different planet entirely.

The same was true with *Music for the Jilted Generation*, which in many way is the most obvious example of Liam's need to break rules. Yet it is also a testament to his ability to explore ideas without becoming contrived or indulgent. At a time when most of the dance scene surrounding him were off making head-trip albums, trying to show their musical genius, Liam succeeded in showing his without ever closing down the access. The tracks remained direct and accessible without becoming safe.

What *The Fat of the Land* does is to succeed in taking this ideology to an absolute extreme. The tracks on the album are the most accessible he has written, yet they're also the most subversive. With an approach to eclecticism which knows no boundaries, he has created a brave statement which stands out on its own. The underlying current of frustration and anger, mixed with cathartic bursts of pure energy help to mark out this album as being the supreme example of the Prodigy vision. Indeed where *Experience* and *Music for the Jilted Generation* successfully summed up their times, *The Fat of the Land* defines the here and now. It is the most modern album of 1997.

Ask the band what they consider to be the main reason for their success, and they would come up with none of the convoluted theorizing of the music critic, they'd simply say that it's because of the amount of work they've put in to their live show. Since their inception in 1991, the band have continuously circumnavigated the world. They've played in the out-of-the-way places as well as the high-profile cities. They've pushed the vibe into as many of the untouched cracks in the globe as possible and, as a result, people everywhere have been able to lock into their rebellion regardless of whether or not they've even heard of the notion of raving. A limited notion which The Prodigy, transcended the minute they first put out a record. They're free-party spirits who send their form of anti-mainstream rebellion straight into the hearts of the world's thrill-seekers.

It's this directness; this absolute now-ness which is possibly the main appeal of The Prodigy. It comes over in their records, it runs through their performance. They are a band who wilfully indulge in the concept of the generation gap, simply because they came from a scene which the entire parent generation attempted to outlaw. The Prodigy are still the renegades. And they will be for a long time to come.

Outro

We're right back where we started. Back in the air. Only this time we're on a private plane returning from Europe and Keith is sauntering down the aisles telling jokes to anyone who'll listen.

Keith loves it on planes. He hands out sandwiches, jokes with the cabin crew and even offers a spot of advice on how to serve coffee without spilling it over the customer. The stewardesses love him. They're also quite enamoured by Maxim who is lying across his seat, feet up on the adjacent chair, cuddling a huge pillow. He's taken this pillow everywhere with him over the past couple of days. It's been the perfect place to rest his weary head . . . and hide it when the need has arisen.

A few rows in front of him, Liam is reading a tabloid, catching up on the news and gossip from back home. He puts the paper down and we start talking about snowboarding again. You can tell he's missing the action of the piste. Of all the band it's he who takes the sport the most seriously, even going to dry slopes as often as possible. And he's counting the days before he can go again.

Up front, Leeroy sits with his legs stretched out. He's in the only seats which will accommodate his lengthy frame. He's knackered. His eyes betray a man who hadn't actually got much sleep the previous night and the turbulence of the plane is testing the limits of his endurance. Until, that is, he discovers that I'm shit scared of flying in these old buckets. It seems unnatural to me that such a rattly old heap could actually get into the air. A jumbo, yes – it's got big engines. But this thing?

Leeroy seizes his chance to tell me a few air flight scare stories – a routine which I later discover is one of his favourite pastimes when there's a journalist along for the ride.

It's still very early in the morning, but within minutes of landing at Essex's Standsted Airport, The Prodigy are surrounded by autograph hunters all begging the band to sign scraps of paper and, in one case, a huge poster of Keith.

'We're not The Prodigy, we're their tribute band,' jokes Keith. But it's no good. They've been rumbled and, just as Leeroy had previously warned me, the fifty-yard walk to the doors takes the boys almost an hour while all around people shout 'Oi, Firestarter' and 'Keith, can we take your photo?' Somewhere in Britain there's someone with pictures of The Prodigy all looking dog-tired. No doubt the photos are taking pride of place on someone's wall. As the band finally manage to leave the airport, I turn to Liam with a final question. The price of fame, or all in a day's work, Liam?

'Hey, we're from round here,' he laughs. 'People are bound to recognize us.'

British Discography

SINGLES

FEBRUARY 1991
'What Evil Lurks' EP
What Evil Lurks/We Gonna Rock/Android/Everybody in the Place

AUGUST 1991
'Charly'
Charly (Alley Cat Mix)/Pandamonium/Your Love/Charly(Original Mix)

DECEMBER 1991
'Everybody in the Place'
Everybody in the Place (Fairground Mix)/Crazy Man/G-Force (Energy Flow)/Rip Up the Soundsystem
• CD version with extra track: Everybody in the Place (Dancehall Version)

SEPTEMBER 1992
'Fire'
Fire (Burning Version)/Fire (Sunrise Version)/Jericho (Original Version)/Jericho (Genaside II Remix)

NOVEMBER 1992
'Out of Space'
Out of Space (Original Mix)/Out of Space (Techno Underworld Mix)/Ruff in the Jungle Bizness (Uplifting Vibes Mix)/Music Reach 1234 (Live)

MARCH 1993
'Wind it Up'

Wind it Up (Rewound)/We are the Ruffest/Weather Experience
• CD version with Weather Experience (Top Buzz Remix)

OCTOBER 1993
'One Love'
One Love (Original Mix)/Rhythm of Life (Original Mix)/Full Throttle
(Original Mix)/One Love (Jonny L Mix)

MAY 1994
'No Good (Start the Dance)'
No Good (Start the Dance)/No Good (Bad For You Mix)/No Good (CJ
Bolland's Museum Mix)/No Good (Original Mix)

AUGUST 1994
'Voodoo People'
Voodoo People (Original Mix)/Voodoo People (Haiti Island Mix)/Voodoo
People (Dust Brothers Mix)/Goa (The Heat the Energy Pt 2)

MARCH 1995
'Poison'
Poison/Rat Poison/Scienide/Poison (Enviromental Science Mix)

FEBRUARY 1996
'Firestarter'
Firestarter/Firestarter (Emperion Mix)/Firestarter (Instrumental)/Molotov
Bitch

JULY 1996
'Mindfields'
Mindfields/Mindfields (Jon Carter Mix)
• Single withdrawn

NOVEMBER 1996
'Breathe'
Breathe (Edit)/Their Law (Live)/Poison (Live)/The Trick

ALBUMS

NOVEMBER 1992
Experience
Jericho/Music Reach 1/2/3/4/Wind it Up/Your Love (Remix)/ Hyperspeed (G-Force Part 2)/Charly (Trip into Drum and Bass Version)/Out of Space/Everybody in the Place (155 and Rising)/Weather Experience/Fire (Sunrise Version)/Ruff in the Jungle Bizness/Death of the Prodigy Dancers (Live)

JULY 1994
Music for the Jilted Generation
Intro/Break and Enter/Their Law (featuring Pop Will Eat Itself)/Full Throttle/Voodoo People/Speedway (theme from the Fast Lane)/The Heat (The Energy)/Poison/No Good (Start the Dance)/One Love (Edit) The Narcotic Suite:/3 Kilos/Skylined/Cluastrophobic Sting

JUNE 1997
The Fat of the Land
Smack My Bitch Up/Breathe/Diesel Power/Funky Shit/Serial Thrilla/ Mindfields/Narayan/Firestarter/Climbatize/Fuel My Fire

OTHER PROJECTS

THE PRODIGY VERSUS TOM MORELLO
One Man Army (on *Spawn* original soundtrack album)

THE LONGMAN
Longman EP (White Label)
The Longman (on *Needs Must* compilation)